A2

CriticalThinking
for OCR

Jo Lally • Colin Hart

www.heinemann.co.uk
✓ Free online support
✓ Useful weblinks
✓ 24 hour online ordering

01865 888058

Heinemann

Inspiring generations

Heinemann Educational Publishers
Halley Court, Jordan Hill, Oxford OX2 8EJ
Part of Harcourt Education

Heinemann is the registered trademark of Harcourt Education Limited

© Harcourt Education 2006

First published 2006

10 09 08 07 06
10 9 8 7 6 5 4 3 2 1

British Library Cataloguing in Publication Data is available
from the British Library on request.

10-digit ISBN: 0 435235850
13-digit ISBN: 978 0 435235 85 7

Typeset by Saxon Graphics

Printed and bound in the UK by Ashford Colour Press, Gosport, Hants

Cover photo: © M.C. Escher's 'Symmetry Drawing E57' © 2005 The M.C. Escher Company-Holland. All rights reserved.

Acknowledgements
Every effort has been made to contact copyright holders of material reproduced in this book, and to ensure information
is correct at the time of printing. However, the publisher will be pleased to rectify any omissions in subsequent printings
if notice is given.

The authors and publisher would like to thank the following individuals and organisations for permission to reproduce
photographs: pp 17, Alamy Images/Ray Roberts; pp 20, Photolibrary/Dynamic Graphics (Uk) Ltd; pp23, Alamy Images/
John Powell Photographer; pp23, Getty Images/ PhotoDisc; pp 35, Photos.com; pp 44, Harcourt Education Ltd. Gareth
Boden; pp 65, Getty Images/ PhotoDisc.

We would like to thank the Office of National Statistics for permission to reproduce the figure on page 29, which is
reproduced under the terms of the Click-Use Licence.

We would like to thank the following people for permission to reproduce copyrighted material: pp 17, © The
Independent, 16 September 2005; pp 23–24, Copyright Guardian Newspapers Limited 2005; pp 27, 65 and 77, New
Scientist; pp 47, Daily Mail; pp 57–58, Copyright Guardian Newspapers Limited 2005; pp 87 and 102, OCR.

Contents

Introduction:
Critical reasoning

What is critical reasoning?

Critical reasoning is an extension of the skills of assessing and developing arguments that you came across at OCR AS Level in Critical Thinking. It can be broken down into the same Assessment Objectives:

- AO1 **Analyse** reasoning
- AO2 **Evaluate** reasoning
- AO3 **Develop** reasoning.

You will analyse reasoning by breaking it down into its component parts.

You will evaluate reasoning by considering the use of evidence and patterns of reasoning to decide whether the reasoning is strong or weak.

You will develop your own reasoning and write well structured and coherent arguments to support a conclusion.

How is critical reasoning at A2 Level different from assessing and developing argument at AS Level?

- You will deal with more advanced topics requiring a further level of thought.
- You will analyse more complex arguments in more detail.
- When you evaluate reasoning you will be expected to relate your points to the overall conclusion of an argument. For example, if you identify a generalisation, you should be able to say whether this means there is no support at all for the conclusion, or whether there are other reasons which still support the conclusion.

- You will develop more complex reasoning, using strands of reasoning, anticipating and responding to counter argument and dealing with subtleties of meaning.

Section 1: Analysing reasoning

Chapter 1: Analysing an argument

In this chapter you will revise and extend your ability to identify elements of an argument. You will revise and extend your understanding of argument structure, and practise a variety of multiple choice questions with a focus on argument analysis.

Chapter 2: Analysing arguments in real sources

Chapter 2 will show you how to apply your analytical skills to real passages. You will learn to spot reasoning and arguments in longer passages which may contain other kinds of writing. You will analyse the outline structure of longer passages and analyse paragraphs of argument in detail. You will practise on texts from newspapers and websites.

Section 2: Evaluating reasoning

Chapter 3: Evaluating evidence, statistics and the visual representation of data

In this chapter you will revise and extend the questioning techniques used at AS Level to evaluate evidence, draw conclusions based on evidence and consider whether evidence strengthens or weakens an argument. You will learn to match verbal and visual descriptions of evidence and argument. You will practise multiple choice questions and extend these skills to the evaluation of evidence in a longer passage, considering the impact of your evaluation on the overall conclusion.

Chapter 4: Evaluating support for a claim: structure of reasoning

In Chapter 4 you will revise and extend your understanding of flaws in the logical structure of reasoning, and consider the implications of flaws in the reasoning for the overall conclusion of a passage.

Chapter 5: Evaluating support for a claim: rhetorical persuasion

In this chapter you will learn to recognise and evaluate rhetorical ploys, including appeals, and their impact on the overall reasoning. You will revise and extend your understanding of the ways in which vague language can affect the support given to a conclusion.

Chapter 6: Evaluating reasoning: counter argument, hypothetical reasoning and analogy

Chapter 6 will show you how to evaluate sustained counter argument and hypothetical reasoning and their impact on the overall reasoning. You will revise and extend your understanding of the role of analogy and hypothetical reasoning in arguments, and practise these skills in multiple choice questions and two longer passages.

Section 3: Developing reasoning

Chapter 7: Developing your own arguments

In Chapter 7 you will apply your improved analytical and evaluative skills to your own reasoning. You will practise writing clear, precise arguments which include complex and subtle reasoning.

Chapter 8: Preparing for the exam

This chapter will explain the general structure of the exam paper and give advice on how to tackle the questions. You will look at worked examples to help you write strong answers.

Chapter 9: Guidance to the activities

This chapter provides answers and/or sample answers for the majority of the activities in Chapters 1–6.

Analysing an argument

Unit 4 is the synoptic unit of your Critical Thinking exam and should bring together all the skills that you have developed during the Critical Thinking course. In Section A you will answer multiple choice questions, and in Section B you will be asked to analyse and evaluate a longer passage of reasoning and develop your own reasoning on a related theme. This chapter will guide you through identifying and analysing arguments. It revises the key terms, concepts and skills covered in more detail in the Unit 2 book, and shows you how to adapt them to the questions you will find in Unit 4.

ACTIVITY ❶

Test yourself. Write a short definition of each of the following terms from your AS Level Critical Thinking course:

Conclusion	Reason	Intermediate conclusion	Assumption
Explanation	Argument	Counter argument	Analogy	Evidence

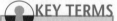

KEY TERMS

Argument – an attempt to persuade an audience (readers or listeners) to accept a conclusion by giving reasons to support that conclusion

KEY TERMS

Explanation – tells how or why something happens but does not persuade listeners or readers to agree with anything

Identifying an argument

An important first step in critical reasoning is learning to identify an **argument**, that is, to tell the difference between arguments and other kinds of writing.

An argument is an attempt to persuade others to accept a conclusion on the basis of reasons which support the conclusion. Sometimes, **explanations** or rhetorical persuasion may look like arguments. However, an explanation does not try to persuade you to agree with anything. For example:

> *Rainfall during the monsoon has decreased in India since the 1950s, despite predictions that global warming would increase it. Although surface temperatures are increasing near the equator, further north the ocean is not warming. It is possible that sunlight is being absorbed by pollution.*

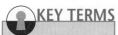

Rhetorical persuasion persuades us emotionally, and does not offer reasons which give strong support to the opinion it is trying to persuade us to agree with. For example:

> *You can't be seen at the party in those. They're so yesterday. Whatever will people think?*

You may also come across rant, which simply gives opinions in a forceful manner but does not offer rational support for those opinions. For example:

> *It is obscene that water companies are making enormous profits at the cost of the ordinary person on the street. They are introducing hosepipe bans while they are letting our water trickle away through their leaky pipes. We have paid for our water and they should deliver it or give us rebates.*

REMEMBER

As you learnt at AS Level Critical Thinking, many arguments, even short ones, include some context or background. This helps readers to know what the argument is about, but it is not part of the argument itself.

Identifying an argument in the Unit 4 exam

You may come across a multiple choice question which asks you to identify one of four passages as an argument. The three wrong answers may be, for example, explanations, expressions of disagreement, random, unconnected sentences or rhetorical attempts to persuade. In section B you will be given one longer passage from a real source. It will be the sort of passage you might find in the comment, analysis and opinion sections of quality newspapers. You will need to be able to separate the argument from context and background, explanation and other forms of writing. We will look at longer passages in more detail in Chapter 2.

ACTIVITY ❷

a) Which of the following is an argument? How would you best describe the other answers?

   A Art should be beautiful. Some works of art only make us think. Too many works of art are ugly.

   B Maggots are a good method of cleaning infected wounds. They eat dead flesh and can reduce the risk of amputation significantly. Maggots can be produced in a sterile way.

   C Light bulbs normally blow when they are first switched on rather than after being used. When it is cold the filament has less resistance, so the electric current surges up it faster when you flick the switch.

D Fitness centres are not interested in helping people improve their fitness. They charge us lots of money and then staff the place with off-puttingly beautiful young people to ensure we daren't turn up.

b) Which one of the following is an argument? How would you best describe the other answers?

A Brain imaging technology should not be used in the courts or by the police or security services. This technology is developing fast. The relationships between brain images and thoughts are very complex.

B The average temperatures between 2000 and 2005 rose despite an increase in cloud cover. Low-lying clouds bounce sunlight away from the earth, whereas high-level clouds trap heat. There have been increasing amounts of high-level cloud.

C In order to be mathematically beautiful, a piece of work must have certain qualities. It must use the minimum number of assumptions, provide an original and important insight or cast new light on existing understanding.

D Scientific research into the paranormal is useful and valuable. This research has not come up with a convincing, reproducible explanation of the paranormal. It has produced some interesting findings about the way the brain works.

KEY TERMS

Reason (R) – normally a general statement which supports a conclusion by giving us grounds or information which helps us to believe, accept or agree with the conclusion

KEY TERMS

Conclusion (C) – a claim which is supported by reasons, which we are supposed to accept after reading an argument

What is the difference between argument and reasoning?

An argument is a rational construction with **reasons** and a **conclusion**. At A2 Level Critical Thinking we will also talk about **reasoning**. Reasoning is a thread of persuasive thought, connected in a logical manner.

- Reasoning can refer to the way the evidence, reasons, assumptions and conclusions are structured and connected in an argument.

- It can also refer to the overall train of thought in a piece which includes arguments and other strategies to persuade the audience to adopt a point of view.

Identifying elements of reasoning in an argument

In this chapter we will concentrate on reasoning in the first sense. We will revise and extend our understanding of how to analyse the reasoning in an argument. That is, we will break arguments down into their parts.

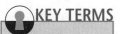 **KEY TERMS**

Reasoning – a thread of persuasive thought, connected in a logical manner

 **REMEMBER**

Remember that we use **R** to mean **Reason**, and **C** to mean **Conclusion** when we are analysing arguments.

Reasons

The simplest form of argument gives one or more reasons to support a conclusion. For example:

> *'It is seven o'clock in the evening. I am hungry. It is time for dinner.'*

This can be broken down as follows:

> R1 It is seven o'clock in the evening.
>
> R2 I am hungry.
>
> C   It is time for dinner.

Remember that something subjective, such as 'I am hungry', can be a perfectly acceptable reason to support a conclusion. An argument which consisted only of opinions would come dangerously close to a rant, but opinions, preferences and subjective claims do have a place in argument.

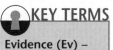 **KEY TERMS**

Evidence (Ev) – facts, figures, statistics and specific information used to support a general reason

Evidence

One way of strengthening an argument is to use **evidence** and examples. Facts, figures, statistics and specific examples can support a general point, or reason, if they are well used. For example:

> *London is a multicultural city. There are 500,000 people of Pakistani origin, 200,000 people of Somali origin and 75,000 people of Chinese origin in the city. There are large communities of worshippers at mosques, synagogues, churches and gurdwaras.*

In this argument, the (fictional) evidence about numbers of people, and examples of different faiths support the claim that London is a multicultural city.

KEY TERMS

Intermediate conclusion (IC) – a claim which is supported by reasons but which gives support to a further conclusion

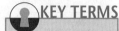

KEY TERMS

Assumption (A) – an unstated step which is essential to an argument

KEY TERMS

Counter argument (CA) – an opposing argument which is shown to be wrong to strengthen the author's argument

Intermediate conclusions

Intermediate conclusions are claims which are supported by reasons, but which give support to a further conclusion. Remember, you can check which is the main conclusion and which is the intermediate conclusion by asking which one gives support to the other.

Assumptions

Assumptions are missing steps in the argument. They are unstated but must be accepted if the conclusion is also to be accepted. It is important to take the time to consider any assumptions underlying an argument. It is often precisely those steps in an argument which are not stated that weaken it.

Counter arguments

Counter arguments put forward an opposing line of reasoning in order to show that it is wrong and so strengthen the author's own argument.

Analysing reasoning

Evidence, reasons, intermediate conclusions, assumptions, counter arguments and conclusions are important structural elements in an argument. You can think of them as the building blocks of reasoning. They can be put together and assembled in different structures. When you are analysing the reasoning in an argument you should simply be identifying which bit is which. It is a labelling exercise to show that you understand how the author's words fit together. This is why you are expected to phrase the elements precisely.

ACTIVITY ③

Identify precisely each structural element in the argument below.

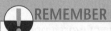

REMEMBER

Remember to include any assumptions you find in your analysis.

> *Research suggests that there is a sleep trigger which slows down in adolescence and makes it difficult for teenagers to go to sleep early. This is also why teenagers struggle to get up early. This means that it is unfair to expect teenagers to attend morning lessons, so schools and colleges should rearrange their working days to start after lunch and finish during the evening.*

KEY TERMS

Principle – a claim which applies beyond the immediate circumstances of an argument and generally provides a guide to action or belief

KEY TERMS

Hypothetical claim – an 'if … then' sentence which looks at the possible consequences of an event or action

KEY TERMS

Analogy – a form of argument which uses parallel situations to encourage the audience to accept a conclusion

Principles, hypothetical claims and analogies

Principles, hypothetical claims and analogies can also be identified when you are analysing the reasoning in an argument.

As you read in Units 2 and 3, **principles** are rule-like claims which apply beyond the immediate circumstances of an argument and generally help us to decide what to do or think. For example, 'All people deserve equal opportunities.' A principle may function as a reason, intermediate conclusion or conclusion in an argument.

Hypothetical claims consider the consequences that may happen if a particular event occurs. They usually take the form, 'if… then.' For example, 'If I don't bother going to work, then my boss will sack me.' Remember to distinguish hypothetical claims which consider 'what if…' from 'even if…' statements. An 'even if' statement, such as 'I'm going to the party even if you're not', defines conditions rather than considering consequences.

Analogies work by saying that two situations are so similar that a conclusion (or reasoning) that can be accepted about one situation should also be accepted about the other. The two situations are said to be parallel. For example:

> *Identifying the structure of an argument is like looking at a skeleton. It helps you to understand how the structure works.*

ACTIVITY ④

Identify precisely each structural element in the argument below. Identify any principles, hypothetical claims or analogies.

> *Freedom of speech is a fundamental part of our democracy. However, we should not abuse this freedom. Being entitled to carry a gun does not entitle you to kill and maim other people at random. So preventing people from persistently ridiculing a group of people, or prohibiting incitement to religious or racial hatred does not go against the principle of free speech. It merely puts civilised limits on its use.*

The structure of reasoning

How reasons support conclusions

In Unit 2 you learnt that reasons should be persuasive, give us good reason to accept a conclusion and be precisely focused on the conclusion. If all these conditions are met, then a reason gives strong support to the conclusion. For example:

> *Being rude about people hurts their feelings. We shouldn't hurt each other's feelings. So it is better not to be rude about someone in their hearing.*

However, if we are persuaded by emotional tricks to agree to something similar but not precisely the same as the conclusion, then the reasoning gives weak support to the conclusion. For example:

> *If you want to look good, you need to dress well. Celebrity X looked good at the Brit Awards. So you should buy the same dress as Celebrity X.*

Here your emotions are being manipulated to make you believe you need to buy a dress. Sometimes writers jump to conclusions without really supporting them, although on first sight their reasoning looks OK. For example:

> *Britons are spending more on leisure and less on food, so we are likely to be getting thinner.*

As we are generally richer, and as food is generally getting cheaper, it is possible to spend less on food yet still eat more than we need. Leisure does not only mean physical activity, so the author has given us no reasons to accept that we might get thinner.

Understanding whether a reason gives precise support to a conclusion is a very important skill in analysing and evaluating an argument. In the short arguments we are dealing with, it may be obvious to you that some of the reasons have little relevance to the conclusion, or that they offer weak support. In a longer argument, this lack of relevance may be hidden by the detail. This is one of the reasons why we identify the structure of an argument.

ACTIVITY ⑤

a) Which of the following would provide strong support for the conclusion that, 'Valentine's Day has greater negative effects than positive'?

  A Valentine's Day is a commercial humbug. Card manufacturers, flower sellers and chocolate makers take our money with fraudulent promises of true love.

  B Suicide rates soar on Valentine's Day as lonely people watch others flaunting their greater success in love and succumb to despair. Others merely cringe as revolting members of the opposite sex plead for their attention.

  C Some people do find or cement lifelong love on Valentine's Day. However, a great many more waste their money on unnecessary gifts which are rejected, or spend a lonely evening on their own. Some even end it all.

  D Valentine's Day is a wonderful celebration of love and generosity and provides a welcome relief from the doom and gloom of everyday life.

b) In which of the following arguments does the reason best support the conclusion?

  A We want our children to be safe. So we should publish lists of known paedophiles living in each community.

  B Anjuli eats at least six portions of fruit and vegetables every day. So she won't get ill.

  C The education of a child is too complex for a single teacher, so we should replace teachers with computer programmes.

  D There is a great deal of suffering in the world, so I should donate some money to a charity such as Oxfam.

 **KEY TERMS**

Strands of reasoning – developed lines of thought, possibly with evidence, examples, reasons and intermediate conclusion(s)

Strands of reasoning

At AS Level Critical Thinking we considered how reasons support a conclusion. At A2, however, we need to extend this understanding to **strands of reasoning**. For example, let's take the following argument:

> R1 *Walking to work is much better for the environment than driving.*
>
> R2 *It is also much better for your health.*
>
> R3 *As you live just a mile from work,*
>
> C   *you should walk to work.*

! REMEMBER

Arrows show the link between reasons and conclusions.

+ and a line are used to show reasons that jointly support a conclusion.

You can refer back to Chapters 1 and 3 in *Critical Thinking for OCR Unit 2* to refresh your memory.

Here we have three simple reasons which support the conclusion independently. We can show this with a simple diagram:

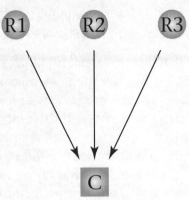

If we wanted to develop the argument, we could make R1 and R2 into intermediate conclusions by supporting them with evidence, examples and additional reasons. This would give us two strands of reasoning as follows:

> *Cars release pollutants such as carbon monoxide into the atmosphere, causing air pollution which leads to acid rain, deforestation and global warming. They also depend on a rapidly depleting stock of fossil fuels, so their use is simply not sustainable. Walking has very little impact on the environment, so **walking to work is much better for the environment than driving**.*
>
> *If you drive to work, you do not use your muscles much. If you walk, you exercise your muscles, get your blood circulating and strengthen your heart. This means you are less likely to suffer heart disease. **So walking to work is better for your health than driving**. As you live just a mile from work, you should walk.*

Now there are two strands of reasoning, one relating to the environment, the other to your health. If you wanted to analyse the argument, you would now have a choice. You could analyse the framework structure. This would produce the simple analysis and diagram we saw above. You might comment on the extra support given to two of the reasons, but would not show it in detail.

Alternatively, you could analyse the reasoning in detail, showing each element, and the complex structure of each strand of the argument. If we took the second paragraph and analysed it in detail it would look like this:

> R1   *If you drive to work, you do not use your muscles much.*
>
> R2   *If you walk, you exercise your muscles, get your blood circulating and strengthen your heart.*
>
> IC   *This means you are less likely to suffer heart disease.*
>
> IC   *So walking to work is better for your health than driving.*
>
> R3   *As you live just a mile from work,*
>
> C   *you should walk.*

There is a role for both framework and detailed analysis. Sometimes we want to clear the detail away and just get an idea of how an argument works to see if it has a strong structure. Sometimes we need to see the details. In both cases, it is important to show how the reasoning supports the main conclusion.

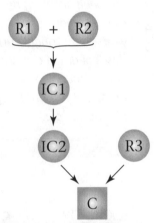

The argument structure in the second paragraph

ACTIVITY ❻

There is an urgent need for a radical shift in the drinking culture in this country. Admissions to hospital for drink-related diseases have almost reached an annual total of 50,000 and drink-related deaths have reached their highest ever level. The reasons for this are the availability of alcohol, the social acceptability of drinking, the increase in women drinkers and the falling price of alcohol. Drink-related violence has also escalated in recent years. For example, 20% of murders and 25% of serious head injuries occur under the influence of alcohol. Our attitude to drink is killing our country.

a) What function does the following element have in the structure of the argument? 'Our attitude to drink is killing our country.'

   A Main conclusion
   B Intermediate conclusion
   C Reason
   D Evidence

b) What function does the following element have in the structure of the argument? 'Drink-related violence has also escalated in recent years.'

   A Main conclusion
   B Intermediate conclusion
   C Reason
   D Evidence

c) Analyse the following argument in detail.

> *Although licensing nurses to prescribe medicines ought to allow people easier access to routine medication, it is a disaster waiting to happen. It takes a doctor more than seven years to thoroughly understand how the human body works, and what effects various doses of drugs can have on it. Nurses do not learn in the same detail. They simply do not know enough to take charge of prescribing drugs. Furthermore, prescription is an unfair burden of responsibility to lay on people who have chosen a caring rather than a diagnostic role.*

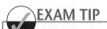 **EXAM TIP**

Practise identifying and analysing arguments you find in the newspapers, in your other subjects and even from AS Critical Thinking exam papers. This will improve your skills. Arguments can be found everywhere.

SUMMARY

You should now be able to:

- identify arguments and explain the difference between arguments, explanations, rants and rhetorical persuasion

- analyse the reasoning in an argument, identifying structural elements such as reasons, conclusions, etc.

- analyse the structure of reasoning, identifying strands of reasoning in an argument.

Analysing arguments in real sources

In this chapter you will extend your analysis skills by dealing with longer passages of reasoning from real life.

Real-life reasoning

A good way to ensure you do the best you can in Critical Thinking exams is to read quality newspapers and magazines to give yourself a good understanding of real-life reasoning. It is worth starting with sections you find interesting, such as sport, fashion, health or family life. Keep a list of new words and read a little bit more each time.

Reasoning in real life includes a variety of strategies to persuade an audience to accept a point of view. In the comment, analysis and opinion sections of a quality newspaper, you will find argument, rhetorical persuasion, explanation and description.

It is a journalist's job to use all of these techniques. It is a critical thinker's job, however, to take a step back and analyse how we are being persuaded to accept a point of view. The critical thinker will assess how strong the rational reasons to accept a conclusion are and won't be swayed only by emotion.

Does emotional persuasion have a role in reasoning?

Should a critical thinker accept that emotional persuasion has a role in reasoning? In real life our emotional reactions are important. All the same, there is a significant difference between agreeing to take into account emotional reactions to an issue and being made to feel so passionate that we accept a conclusion which has no rational support or act without considering reasons.

So we will consider the role of rhetorical persuasion and its place in reasoning. When we identify that a journalist has used emotional appeals which give little rational support to their conclusion, we are not saying that a journalist has done a bad job. We are simply looking at their article in a very particular way.

In this chapter, however, our focus will remain on the rational support for a conclusion. We will start by looking at the *framework of reasoning*, and move on to *analysing in detail*.

Analysing the framework of reasoning

Identifying the main conclusion in a longer text

EXAM TIP

Another way to help check your decision is to look at the subheading of the article. It may paraphrase the main conclusion. However, it may simply summarise the article, or quote a striking phrase, so don't trust it completely. Use the subheading as an aid which might help your own decision.

The first thing to do when analysing a text is to identify the main conclusion. At Critical Thinking A2, when using real texts, the task of identifying the main conclusion may be complicated. The argument may have a complex structure, with a number of strands of reasoning and more than one intermediate conclusion. If the article ends with an intermediate conclusion, it can be tempting to pick that instead of the main conclusion. Remember to test your decision by checking whether the element you have decided on is actually supported by all the other elements of the reasoning.

In real-life texts authors do not always state their main conclusion. Look out for this when you are reading, and practise drawing their conclusion precisely for them.

Identifying the reasons and conclusion in a longer text

Let's look at a medium-length text which appeared in *The Independent*, 16 September 2005. It has a lovely, clear structure. Try to identify the main conclusion, and reasons which support the main conclusion before you read the analysis.

REMEMBER

Remember that a reason which gives support to the main conclusion in the framework structure is usually supported by evidence and other reasons, so it is often an intermediate conclusion. You can refresh your memory on this in Chapter 3 of *Critical Thinking for OCR Unit 2*.

Public Art – A powerful and positive image

Marc Quinn's sculpture of Alison Lapper

Marc Quinn's **1** sculpture of Alison Lapper, officially unveiled on the fourth plinth of Trafalgar Square yesterday, is now one of the most striking sights in London. Ms Lapper was born with no arms and shortened legs as a result of a congenital disorder. In Quinn's sculpture, she is depicted eight months pregnant and naked. It is a powerful and positive image. As the artist himself puts it: 'It is so rare to see disability in everyday life – let alone naked, pregnant and proud.'

Those perplexed by the notion of a **2** disabled person on a pedestal might bear in mind that Nelson, whose own monument adorns the same square, had one arm. The sculpture is also a clever echo of those revered icons of antiquity such as the *Venus de Milo* and the *Apollo Belvedere,* neither of which is considered ugly because of its missing limbs. The sculpture provokes thoughts on heroism too. According to the Mayor of London, Ken Livingstone, whose office underwrote this project: 'This square celebrates the courage of men in battle. Alison's life is a struggle to overcome much greater difficulties than many of the men we celebrate and commemorate here.'

Not all will agree with this. But the **3** virtue of the sculpture is that it encourages people to address such issues. Some have taken issue with Quinn's workmanship, calling *Alison Lapper Pregnant* a 'concept' rather than a sculpture. But this is a side issue. It is true that Quinn's work was created with moulds. But so were the bronzes of Henry Moore, which adorn many a public space. And we must be careful not to be drawn into a sterile debate about the merits of conceptual art.

Regardless of whether people like this **4** artwork aesthetically or not, it has generated a welcome debate about public sculpture and what it is for. From Antony Gormley's iron figures in Liverpool to Millennium Square in Bristol, public art in Britain is capturing the imagination. Giancarlo Neri's sculpture of a giant table and chair on Hampstead Heath has become a focal point for the local community in a way that few anticipated.

Controversy was recently generated **5** over a rock sculpture called *Monolith and Shadow* commissioned to stand outside a new London hospital. It was described as a '£70,000 pebble' by the down-market press. But this only served to demonstrate their knowledge of the price of everything and the value of nothing. Public art, whether commissioned by the public or private sector, has the capacity to enhance our cities and our quality of life. *Alison Lapper Pregnant* is a welcome addition to our capital's collection of artistic riches.

Source: **The Independent,** *16 September 2005*

The main conclusion of this article is, '*Alison Lapper Pregnant* is a welcome addition to our capital's collection of artistic riches.'

The framework of the argument can be analysed as follows:

> R1   *It is a powerful and positive image.*
>
> R2   *(Assumed reason.) Images of disability or of people who lack limbs can be beautiful and important.*
>
> R3   *The sculpture provokes thoughts on heroism too.*
>
> IC   *The virtue of the sculpture is that it encourages people to address such issues (disability, beauty, heroism).*
>
> R4   *We must be careful not to be drawn into a sterile debate about the merits of conceptual art.*
>
> R5   *It (the statue) has generated a welcome debate about public sculpture and what it is for.*
>
> R6   *Public art has the capacity to enhance our cities and our quality of life.*
>
> C   Alison Lapper Pregnant *is a welcome addition to our capital's collection of artistic riches.*

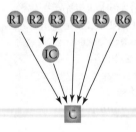

Note that R2 is not stated explicitly. It is an assumption. The author uses comparisons with other works of art and clearly implies, but does not state, that images of disability can be beautiful and important. The diagram in the margin shows the framework of the argument.

Analysing the reasoning in detail

Once the framework of the structure has been identified, parts of the reasoning can be analysed in detail. Remember that a reason for the main conclusion will probably be supported by other reasons and evidence, and is therefore called an intermediate conclusion in a detailed analysis. So something labelled R1 in the framework structure will probably have a different label, usually IC, in the detailed structure analysis. Let's look at paragraph 2:

R1   (Analogy) Those perplexed by the notion of a disabled person on a pedestal might bear in mind that Nelson, whose own monument adorns the same square, had one arm.

R2   The sculpture is also a clever echo of those revered icons of antiquity

Ex   such as the Venus de Milo and the Apollo Belvedere,

R3   neither of which is considered ugly because of its missing limbs.

IC1   (Assumed R2 from main structure) Images of disability or which lack limbs can be beautiful and important.

R4   The sculpture provokes thoughts on heroism too.

Ex   According to the Mayor of London, Ken Livingstone, whose office underwrote this project: 'This square celebrates the courage of men in battle. Alison's life is a struggle to overcome much greater difficulties than many of the men we celebrate and commemorate here.'

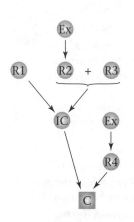

We can draw a diagram to show the detailed analysis of paragraph 2 and the way it supports the main conclusion.

Alternatively, we could use words instead of a diagram. We could say: R1 and R3 combine to support IC1. IC1 and R4 independently support the claim that the virtue of the sculpture is that it encourages people to address such issues.

ACTIVITY

Analyse in detail paragraph 5 of the article about *Alison Lapper Pregnant* **on page 17.**

✓ **EXAM TIP**

In the exam you will not have time to analyse the framework structure of a long, complex article. Instead, you are likely to be given questions in Section B which point you to key parts of the argument, and ask you to identify and explain their function in the structure of the argument. You are also likely to be asked to analyse a shorter part of the reasoning in detail.

Putting the skills into practice

Let's look at a long article:

Who says nuclear power is clean?

Three massive claims are being made for Britain building a new generation of nuclear stations: firstly, it is the only way that Britain can meet its ambitious targets for reducing carbon emissions; secondly, it is the only reliable option available if we are to fill the energy gap left by declining sources of fossil fuels; thirdly it is the best way of ensuring that our energy comes from 'secure' sources, rather than unstable oil-rich oligarchies. **1**

The cooling towers of a nuclear power station

These claims are at best specious, at worst untrue. Take carbon emission. There is a blithe notion that nuclear power is 'clean' – it emits no CO_2 and therefore does not contribute to global warming. This argument has been systematically taken apart over the past five years by two independent experts, one a chemist and energy specialist, the other a nuclear physicist. They have looked at the entire life cycle of a nuclear power station, from the mining of the uranium to the storage of the resulting nuclear waste. Their conclusions make grim reading for any nuclear advocate. **2**

They say that, at the present rate of use, worldwide supplies of rich uranium ore will soon become exhausted, perhaps within the next decade. Nuclear power stations of the future will have to rely on second-grade ore, which requires huge amounts of conventional energy to mine it. For each tonne of poor-quality uranium, some 5000 tonnes of granite will have to be mined, milled and then disposed of. This could rise to 10,000 tonnes if the quality deteriorates further. At some point, and it could happen soon, the nuclear industry will be emitting as much carbon dioxide from mining and treating its ore as it saves from the 'clean' power it produces thanks to nuclear fission. **3**

At this stage, according to an article by the energy writer Fleming, 'nuclear power production would go into energy deficit. It would be putting more energy into the process than it could extract from it. Its contribution to meeting the world's energy needs would become negative.' The so-called 'reliability' of nuclear power would therefore rest on the growing use of fossil fuels rather than their replacement. **4**

Worse, the number of nuclear plants needed to meet the world's needs would be colossal. At present, about 440 reactors supply about 2% of demand. The Massachusetts Institute of Technology calculates that 1000 more would be needed to raise this even to 10% of need. At this point, the search for new sources of ore would become critical. Where would they come from? Not friendly Canada, which produces most of it at present, but places like Kazakhstan, hardly the most stable of democracies. So much for 'secure' sources of energy. We would find ourselves out of the oil-producing frying pan, right in the middle of the ore-manufacturing fire. **5**

These arguments have to be met before other, more searching questions are answered   6
about where we intend to store waste, what we are going to do to prevent radioactive leaks,
and how we should protect nuclear plants against terrorism. The truth is that this form of
energy is, in the end, no more safe, reliable or clean than the others. That does not mean
turning our backs on it: it means confronting reality rather than myth.

The decision to go nuclear will make the case for renewable energy stronger rather than   7
weaker. There has been a growing sense that the Government has lost faith in wind, wave and
tidal power, on the grounds that the public has turned against them and that their efficiency is
doubtful. Wind turbines in particular have been subjected to sustained local campaigns and
derisive columns from the pro-nuclear lobby. They have one great advantage, however – they
are genuinely reversible. A wind turbine, unlike a nuclear reactor, can be removed once it has
come to the end of its natural life.

Nor, in comparison to nuclear power are they gravely inefficient. Of course, a wind farm   8
depends on wind, which may or may not blow, and a wave machine is similarly weather-
dependent. But both need to be part of Britain's energy jigsaw. It is absurd, for instance, that
the Government is withholding the £50 million investment that is needed to turn wave power
into a commercial proposition. Experiments in the Orkney Islands have proved so promising
that the Portuguese government has bought the technology.

The British Government must not exclude options other than nuclear power. Nuclear is not   9
trouble free, and the more you look at it, the more enticing the other choices become.

Source: Magnus Linklater, **The Times,** *23 November 2005*

We can see that the author first counters the idea that nuclear power
is clean, reliable and secure. He then adds that there are safety issues.
The next strand of argument shows two ways in which wind, wave
and tidal power seem attractive in comparison with nuclear power.
These two strands support the intermediate conclusion, 'Nuclear is
not trouble free, and the more you look at it, the more enticing the
other choices become', which directly supports the main conclusion.

An exam question might ask:

*Identify and briefly explain the function of the following elements in
the structure of the argument:*

*a) These would not come from friendly Canada but places like
    Kazakhstan*

b) These (three) claims are at best specious, at worst untrue.

*c) The British Government must not exclude options other than
    nuclear power.*

a) Is a reason to support the intermediate conclusion, 'so much for secure sources of energy.'

b) Is an intermediate conclusion which brings together the first three strands of reasoning and gives support to the main conclusion.

c) Is the main conclusion.

We will return to this article in later chapters. We will evaluate the use of evidence (Chapter 3), the quality of reasoning (Chapters 4 and 5) and counter argument (Chapter 6). We will use it in Chapter 7 as a basis for developing your own reasoning.

ACTIVITY 8

Analyse in detail paragraph 3 of the article on nuclear power on pages 20–21.

ACTIVITY 9

a) Research different forms of energy.

b) Debate their advantages and disadvantages in class.

c) Write letters to a newspaper putting forward your arguments about nuclear or other power.

d) Analyse your own reasoning and make a display, using different colours for reasons, intermediate conclusions and main conclusion.

ACTIVITY ⑩

Read the following article and answer the questions on page 24.

Consumer capitalism is making us ill – we need a therapy state

Britain is becoming unhappier as depression, crime and alcoholism grow. Government can and should intervene. **1**

Britain may have got very much richer in the past 40 years but it has not got happier. In fact, by measures such as depression, crime, obesity, and alcoholism, we have got very much unhappier. **2**

Research has established more clearly than ever what the most likely predictors of happiness are, and there are now proven methods to treat unhappiness. Happiness is no longer an elusive, fuzzy feeling: a body of data gives us the tools to analyse what it is and what causes it. Happiness has gone respectable, and it's been tagged to intellectual disciplines – the science of happiness, happiness economics – so it will be taken more seriously. **3**

But there is an even more pressing reason to take happiness seriously – unhappiness is an expensive business. Mental ill health is the biggest single cause of incapacity and costs the country an estimated £9 billion in lost productivity and benefits. The weight on the NHS is enormous. **4**

Plus, there is a whole range of political issues which have roots in mental health, from **5** obesity and alcoholism, to parenting, the respect agenda and antisocial behaviour among children and young people.

The old liberal concept that the emotional life of citizens is no business of the state is crumbling. This raises the prospect of a future politics where emotional wellbeing could be as important a remit of state public health policy as our physical wellbeing. In 10 years' time, alongside 'five fruit and veg a day,' our kids could be chanting comparable mantras for daily emotional wellbeing: do some exercise, do someone a good turn, count your blessings, laugh, savour beauty. **6**

We might also be discussing emotional pollution in much the way we now discuss environmental pollution. Top of the list would be advertising, which is bad for our emotional health. It induces dissatisfaction with its invidious comparisons with an affluent elite. There would also be a strong rationale to increase subsidies for festivals, parks, theatres, community groups, amateur dramatics, choirs and sports clubs. **7**

To some, these kinds of interventions represent a nightmare scenario of a nanny state, an unacceptable interference in personal freedom. If people want to pursue their own unhappiness, then the state has no right to stop them. **8**

But the problem is, as Richard Layard argues in his book *Happiness: Lessons from a New Science*, that the decline of both religious belief (a strong predictor of happiness) and the social solidarity movements of the 20th century has left a vacuum of understanding about what constitutes a good life and how to be happy.   **9**

The church has lost sway, and the state has retreated behind the single rationale of promoting economic competitiveness with its overtones of Darwinian selection (a major source of unhappiness in itself with its vision of life as a competitive struggle). That leaves the market a free rein to describe happiness –   **10**

the new car, new sofa, new holiday – and to manipulate our insecurities around status.

Leave things as they are and the state will increasingly have to pick up the bill for how consumer capitalism effectively produces emotional ill health – depression, stress, anxiety. Leave things as they are and the state is part of the problem, promoting a set of market values that produce emotional pollution. The state should resume a role in promoting the good life, not just chivvy us along in the global rat race, anxious and insecure.   **11**

Source: Madeleine Bunting, **The Guardian,** *5 December 2005*

a) Identify and briefly explain the function of the following elements in the structure of the reasoning:

   i)   So happiness will be taken more seriously.

   ii) To some, these kinds of intervention represent a nightmare scenario of a nanny state.

   iii) The state has retreated behind the single rationale of promoting economic competitiveness.

   iv) The state should resume a role in promoting the good life, not just chivvy us along in the global rat race, anxious and insecure.

b) Analyse in detail paragraph 7.

As with the article on nuclear power, we will return to this article about happiness in later chapters.

REMEMBER

Remember to show an understanding of different strands of argument.

SUMMARY

You should now be able to:

- analyse the framework structure of the reasoning, identifying and explaining the function of key elements in the structure

- analyse a short piece of reasoning in detail

- feel more comfortable working with real-life reasoning.

Evaluating evidence, statistics and the visual representation of data

In this chapter we will extend your understanding of how to evaluate the use of evidence. We will build on the concepts from *Critical Thinking for OCR Unit 2* Chapter 4, and *Critical Thinking for OCR Unit 3* Chapter 1. You should already be comfortable with the skills of:

- drawing conclusions and making inferences from evidence
- identifying additional evidence needed to verify a claim
- looking for plausible explanations of evidence
- understanding whether additional evidence strengthens or weakens an argument
- evaluating evidence in terms of how reliable, representative and relevant it is.

We will revise these skills and show how they may be tested in multiple choice questions. We will add the skill of matching verbal and visual representations. We will also look in greater detail at the evaluation of evidence in a longer passage, concentrating on the use of evidence to support sustained reasoning. Our main question will always be whether the evidence is precisely focused on the claim it supports.

Drawing conclusions and making inferences

Infer and **draw a conclusion** are different ways of saying the same thing. If we look at reasons or evidence and decide which conclusions can be supported by these reasons or this evidence, we are making an inference, or drawing a conclusion. In this chapter we will focus on drawing conclusions and making inferences from evidence, but the same process can be used with reasons as well.

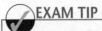

EXAM TIP

Multiple choice questions may ask either, 'Which of the following can reliably be inferred from the evidence?' or, 'Which of the following can be concluded from the evidence?' Both questions mean that you have to work out the next step in the argument.

How certain are inferences?

There is a very strict sense of inference, where we say, 'X is the case, what *must* also be the case?'

For example, what can be inferred from the following information?

> *Sparrows are birds. Birds have wings.*

Here we can infer that sparrows have wings. It is not very interesting, but it must be the case. It is difficult to think of many examples in everyday life which allow us to draw certain conclusions that we don't already know. There is almost always a gap in our knowledge or an element of uncertainty which means that we can only look at what is probable.

Let's look at another example:

> *The tide is coming in fast. You are having a picnic well below the tide line.*

What can we infer here? Well, we can be sure that if you stay where you are you will get wet. You may be swept up by the incoming tide. We cannot be sure of this, but it is possible. It depends on the tidal range, the strength of the tide and how quickly you react when you notice what is happening. If you cannot swim (or cannot swim well fully dressed in tidal waters) you may need to be rescued, or you may drown. None of this is as certain as our inference in the previous example, that sparrows must have wings. On the other hand, it is probable that you are in danger, and that this less certain reasoning will have consequences for your life and health which matter far more than the certainty that sparrows have wings.

ACTIVITY ⓫

What can you infer from the evidence below? How certain do you think it is?

a) The kettle is boiling. Funmilola has spilled water from the kettle on her arm.

b) The throttle on Kamal's car is stuck open. The brakes have failed.

What can be inferred from evidence?

If we can infer something, we can say it follows from the evidence. Let's take another piece of evidence:

> *50% of faulty gadgets returned to shops turned out to be too complex for their users to operate.*
>
> *Source:* New Scientist, *15 March 2006*

What follows from this? Let's take four options:

- 50% of people are stupid.
- Gadgets should be simpler.
- We don't need such complex gadgets.
- Clearer instructions are needed.

50% of people are stupid. We definitely cannot conclude this. The evidence that 50% of 'faulty' gadgets are simply too complex for their users does not mean that these users are stupid. We cannot use a statistic about 50% of 'faulty' gadgets to draw a conclusion about 50% of people. We do not know what percentage of people who have bought gadgets have returned them. It may be a very small proportion. It's also possible that some of them may be highly intelligent but baffled by gadgetry.

Gadgets should be simpler. This seems to be a safer inference. If people cannot use their gadgets, then perhaps these gadgets should be simpler so that people can use them. However, there are a couple of problems with this. Again, we do not know what percentage of people who have bought gadgets have returned them. If 99% of people who buy gadgets are able to use them, 1% return them, and half of those find them too complex, then perhaps there is not a strong case for gadgets to be simpler. We also need to question what is meant by simpler. Do we mean that they should have simpler functions? There may be a good case for retaining the complexity of function because it is useful to those who can cope with it. Or do we mean that gadgets should retain the same functions but be simpler to use? This would be a safer conclusion. Perhaps, then, we could conclude that it would be a good idea if gadgets were simpler to use.

We don't need such complex gadgets. This claim is far too strong to be concluded from the evidence that 50% of 'faulty' gadgets are too complex for their users. We may well need things that are complex.

Clearer instructions are needed. This seems to be quite reasonable. However, we would need to know how clear the instructions for these gadgets are before making a claim that they should be clearer.

So, it seems that the best conclusion we have come to is that it would be a good idea if gadgets were simpler to use – or perhaps more user friendly.

ACTIVITY ⓬

Drugs which can erase specific memories will be available within 10 years.

a) Which of the following is a conclusion that can be drawn from the evidence?

  A No one will have to live with memories of traumatic events.

  B It will be important to decide whether these drugs are ethically acceptable.

  C Bad memories are important in making decisions about future actions.

  D Memory alteration will change what it means to be a human being.

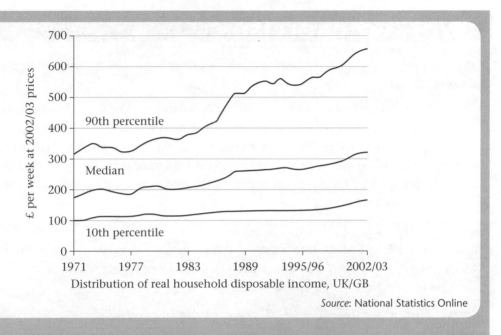

Distribution of real household disposable income, UK/GB

Source: National Statistics Online

b) Which of the following can reliably be inferred from the graph?

   A Disposable income has risen less for the richest than the poorest.

   B Fewer people have control of the nation's wealth.

   C Standards of living have risen generally while the income gap has grown.

   D Standards of living have decreased for the poor, and increased for the rich.

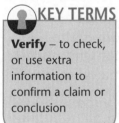

KEY TERMS

Verify – to check, or use extra information to confirm a claim or conclusion

Additional information to verify a claim/conclusion

Our discussion of what can be concluded from a piece of evidence shows that one piece of evidence is rarely enough to support a conclusion. We normally need additional information or evidence. In the example about gadgets, it was quickly evident that we needed to know what percentage of people who buy gadgets return them as faulty. We can talk about using additional information to **verify** a conclusion.

ACTIVITY ⑬

Look again at Activity 11 on page 27. Consider the conclusions you drew. What additional information do you need to verify your conclusions?

Worked exercise

Look at the following example. Try to work out the answer before reading through the discussion.

> Top of the range cars are to have systems which automatically contact emergency services if the car crashes. When the airbag opens, the system sends the car's location to a call centre, using mobile phone technology. An operator asks through a loudspeaker on the dashboard if the driver needs help. If the driver does not respond, paramedics are sent to the scene.

Which piece of additional information, which might be available from the car's onboard computer, would be most useful to operators in deciding whether paramedics should be sent to the scene?

   A Whether the driver remains in the car after the accident.

   B Whether the driver was wearing a seatbelt at the time of the accident.

   C Whether the driver was talking on a mobile phone at the time of the accident.

   D Whether many vehicles were involved in the crash.

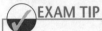

EXAM TIP

In this question you need to know that wearing a seatbelt or not affects your chances of being injured in a crash. In the exam you won't be expected to have specialist knowledge, but you may be expected to have common knowledge like this.

The right answer is B. Whether a driver is wearing a seatbelt during an accident is one of the key factors which influences whether a driver suffers serious head injury.

A looks like a good answer. If the driver is in the car but not responding, then serious injury is likely. However, a driver who has been ejected from the car will also have serious injuries. On the other hand, a driver who has got out of the car to shout at the other driver probably has less need of paramedics.

C would be useful to the police in deciding whether to prosecute a driver, but would make little difference to the need for paramedics.

D would make a difference to how many paramedics might be needed rather than whether to send them.

ACTIVITY ⑭

Chocolate: the new oil?

We all know about the energy in chocolate that so readily converts to fat on our hips. Research now suggests that the energy from chocolate waste could help keep our cars on the road. A team of researchers fed bacteria sugary waste from a chocolate factory. The bacteria ate the sugar and produced hydrogen. This hydrogen was used to power a fuel cell which generated enough energy to drive a small fan.

Which of the following would be needed to verify the claim that chocolate waste could help keep our cars on the road?

A How far the researchers had to transport the chocolate waste.

B How much chocolate waste was needed to power the fan.

C Whether more energy was produced than was used to make the chocolate.

D Whether hydrogen-powered fuel cells are widely available.

Evidence to strengthen or weaken an argument

We have looked at finding additional evidence to verify a claim or conclusion. A related skill is deciding whether an additional piece of evidence might strengthen or weaken an argument, or whether it does neither. If additional evidence would support a claim, such as a reason or intermediate conclusion, it will strengthen the argument. If it would provide support for a counter claim or counter argument, the evidence will weaken an argument.

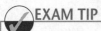
EXAM TIP

At AS Level of the Critical Thinking course you might have come across questions which ask you whether evidence strengthens or weakens an argument. At A2 Level, in addition to these questions, you may be asked which possible answer neither weakens nor strengthens an argument or some reasoning.

ACTIVITY ⓞ

'Abortion should be discouraged.'

Separate the evidence below into three columns: evidence which strengthens the claim that abortion should be discouraged; evidence which weakens the claim; and evidence which neither strengthens nor weakens the claim.

a) The fertilised egg holds the DNA of a human being. So do nail clippings.

b) Identical twins are one entity at the point of fertilisation.

c) The vast majority of fertilised eggs are discarded naturally through miscarriage.

d) The risks of abortion include infection, haemorrhage and problems with future pregnancies.

e) Women are four times as likely to die in the year following an abortion as in the year following a birth.

f) Pregnant women are at lower risk of ill health because they adopt healthier behaviour to protect the child.

g) The risk of death from early abortion is no more than one-seventh the risk during childbirth or full-term pregnancy.

h) Teenage mothers have an increased risk of depression.

i) Women are more likely to suffer from depression, bipolar disorder and drug abuse following an abortion.

ACTIVITY ⓰

a) Write an argument of about 80–100 words which supports or challenges the claim that abortion should be discouraged.

b) Turn your short argument into a multiple choice question. Consider which question type would be best for your argument, e.g. 'Which of the following most strengthens the argument?' Write one right answer and three wrong (but tempting!) answers. Analyse your argument, and provide a brief justification of why your answer is right and why the other possible answers are wrong. Remember that anyone doing your question should have to think quite hard to find the right answer.

ACTIVITY ⓱

> There is a world of tiny microelectromechanical (MEM) machines that are measured in micro- and nanometres. Engineers must understand the differences between this mesoscopic* world and our own. The accelerometers that trigger air-bags in a car crash are mesoscopic, MEM devices. Digital light projectors are also controlled by mesoscopic chips. There is a kind of mesoscopic xylophone which vibrates when struck with radio waves. Because they can be carved directly into the silicon phone circuitry, these tiny xylophones may replace conventional receivers.
>
> *Mesoscopic: very small, measured in micro- and nanometres.

Which of the following, if true, would neither strengthen nor weaken the support for the claim that, 'engineers must understand the differences between this mesoscopic world and our own'?

A The same electrostatic forces which stick a party balloon to the ceiling could root a mesoscopic wheel to the spot.

B At mesoscopic levels, the forces between atoms and molecules are more significant than at human scale.

C Most engineers will probably continue working on human scale rather than mesoscopic devices.

D Mesoscopic submarines may one day explore our bodies from the inside, carrying out repairs.

Looking for plausible explanations of evidence

We have looked at drawing conclusions from evidence – looking at ideas which can be supported by evidence. Sometimes, instead of looking at the next step in an argument, we are concerned with why the evidence is the way it is. For example, we know that trees grow taller at the bottom of mountains than at the top. We want an explanation of why this is the case. It might be that there is more soil on lower slopes, which gives trees more nutrients.

Let's take an example:

Worked example

> *Many of the great modern philosophers are women who studied during the Second World War – Mary Midgely, Iris Murdoch, Elizabeth Anscombe, Philippa Foot and Mary (now Baroness) Warnock. This was the first generation of women to rise to prominence in academic work.*

Which of the following, if true, best explains the evidence?

A The absence of men during the war allowed these women to develop their own voice.

B Women are generally less good at philosophy than men so they could only do well if the men were away.

C Previous generations of women were not interested in philosophy.

D Many women married early rather than studying subjects like philosophy in case their sweethearts did not come home.

A best explains the evidence. Without the dominant presence of males, it is possible that these young women were able to develop their own way of thinking. This is certainly how Mary Midgely explains the rise of this generation of women philosophers.

B. This would not explain why the women continued to do well after the return of the men and became great philosophers alongside their male peers.

C. The interests of previous generations of women would not explain how this generation became great philosophers; it would only explain why previous women had not become philosophers.

D. This would explain why fewer rather than more women excelled in academic study.

ACTIVITY 18

Two groups of students were studied. One group used a vertical classroom, in which students stood at desks with laptops, and were encouraged to walk around the room. The other group used a conventional classroom. The group in the vertical classroom burned more calories during the school day. The group in the conventional classroom gained less weight.

Which of the following would NOT explain the evidence?

A The group in the conventional classroom participated in more sport during the evening.

B The group in the conventional classroom ate bigger meals during the evening.

C The group in the vertical classroom ate bigger meals during the evening.

D The group in the vertical classroom participated in less sport during the evening.

Matching verbal and visual descriptions

Information is often presented visually, perhaps as a graph, table or diagram. It is a useful skill to be able to match verbal and visual descriptions. You may come across a multiple choice question which tests this skill. Let's take an example:

Worked exercise

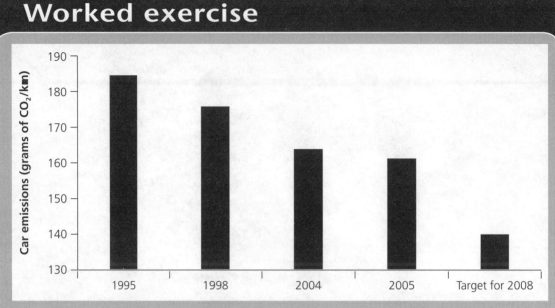

CO_2 emissions by new cars

Which of the following descriptions best matches the information in the bar chart?

A Emissions by new cars are decreasing at a steady rate and are likely to meet the target of 140g/km by 2008.

B Emissions by new cars are decreasing at a steady rate but are unlikely to meet the target of 140g/km by 2008.

C Emissions by new cars are decreasing, but not at a steady rate, and are unlikely to meet the target of 140g/km by 2008.

D Emissions by new cars are decreasing, but not at a steady rate, and are likely to meet the target of 140g/km by 2008.

In this case the answer is C. Emissions are decreasing, but the rate of decrease is slowing down, as far as we can tell from the information, so it is not a steady rate. Because the rate of decrease is slowing down, it seems unlikely that the target will be met.

Evidence in longer arguments

We have looked in some detail at the various kinds of multiple choice question which might test your understanding of the use of evidence in an argument. We now need to look at the use of evidence in a

**KEY TERMS**

Relevance – has special meaning in Critical Thinking. It means something which is precisely focused on the reason or conclusion it is supporting. Just being about the same topic does not make information relevant to the conclusion

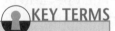**KEY TERMS**

Reliable evidence – evidence that comes from a source which is reputable, authoritative and without a clear vested interest to mislead

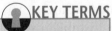**KEY TERMS**

Representative evidence – evidence based on a sample which is large enough for the results to be applied more generally

passage of sustained reasoning. Our focus will be on the **relevance** of the evidence to the precise points the author is making.

We will also consider whether the evidence is **reliable** or **representative**, because both of these issues affect the strength of the evidence, as discussed in Units 1, 2 and 3. For example:

> *According to pharmaceutical giants, DrugsUR, animal testing is a vital part of developing new medicines and protecting the general public from side effects. Moreover, a study they commissioned indicates that 89% of the population is in fact in favour of animal testing.*

DrugsUR would have a strong vested interest in people accepting animal testing. They should be authoritative on the need for some testing, but their vested interest probably outweighs this. The study was commissioned by them, but we do not know who the sample group was – employees, perhaps? We cannot be sure that these results can really be extended to the general population. So this evidence does not give strong support to a conclusion about animal testing being either necessary or popular.

There are two approaches to evaluating evidence in a longer passage. You could either start from a general evaluative comment, and give examples to support your evaluation, or you could comment on the strength of individual uses of evidence and build up to an evaluation of the use of evidence in a passage. While you are practising and learning the skills, it may be a good idea to build up a picture slowly by concentrating on each piece of evidence. In an exam, however, you are unlikely to have time to make a comment about each piece of evidence. In these circumstances, you would be better off taking an overview, and picking out key pieces of evidence to support your view. We will concentrate on this second method.

Let's work through the text, 'Who thinks nuclear power is clean?' on pages 20–21 in Chapter 2 and consider the use of evidence.

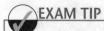

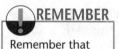

The author makes precise, relevant and reliable use of evidence to support his claims that nuclear power is not clean, reliable or secure. The sources in paragraph 2 – a chemist and energy specialist and a nuclear physicist – are claimed to be expert and independent, so we expect their evidence to be reliable. The author uses this evidence to show that, although the production of nuclear power may be clean in terms of CO_2 production, the whole process including mining, refining and transportation of ore is increasingly polluting. The evidence he uses precisely undermines the claim that nuclear power is clean. The evidence also shows precisely that nuclear power is no more reliable than fossil fuels, because the process depends on the use of fossil fuels.

However, the demonstration that nuclear power is not secure depends on an unsupported leap. The author tells us that Canada will not be the source of future uranium ore, but that we must rely on unstable, undemocratic countries. In order to accept this claim we would need to know that Canada has very limited supplies; we need to know whether all the countries which might provide ore are unstable or unfriendly; and we must assume that this instability will continue into the future. This link then, although precise, rests on gaps in the evidence and rhetorical moves rather than rational, persuasive use of evidence.

Evidence is used rather more loosely to persuade the reader that the decision to go nuclear will make the case for renewable energy stronger rather than weaker. Each piece of evidence acts as an example rather than to give direct support to claims. The claim that wind turbines, unlike nuclear reactors, can be removed, does make wind turbines seem attractive. It does not necessarily, however, affect the strength of the case for renewable energy.

No evidence is given to support the claim th
gravely inefficient in comparison to nuclear po
claim which clearly could and should be support
evidence. The example of the Portuguese governme
technology may be good; Portugal, like Britain, has a
coastline. The fact that a government has bought into te
gives it credibility. On the other hand, even governments
poor decisions; British decisions should be made on the meri
technology, rather than based on other governments' decisions

Overall then, the use of evidence to debunk the claims about nuclea
power is fairly strong; the use of evidence to support the claims
relating to renewable power is patchy, reliant on examples and stray
scraps of evidence.

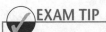

EXAM TIP

A good evaluation of the strength of evidence refers to specific claims, and comments on how well the evidence gives support to that particular claim.

ACTIVITY ⓚ

Read the text, 'Consumer capitalism is making us ill – we need a therapy state' on pages 23–24 in Chapter 2. Evaluate the support given to the author's claims by the use of evidence.

SUMMARY

You should now be able to:

- draw conclusions and make inferences from evidence
- identify additional evidence needed to verify a claim
- find plausible explanations of evidence
- understand to what extent additional evidence strengthens or weakens an argument
- match verbal and visual representations
- evaluate the use of evidence in a longer passage.

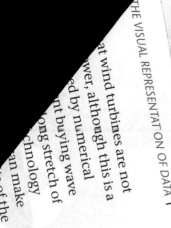

THE VISUAL REPRESENTATION OF DATA

at wind turbines are not
...wer, although this is a
...ed by numerical
...nt buying wave
...ong stretch of
...chnology
...an make
...s of the

...f Critical Thinking is evaluating how well a piece
...s a claim (usually an intermediate or main
...ter 3 we looked at evaluating the use of evidence
...hapter we will consider ways of evaluating the
...reasoning to see whether a particular claim is well
supported. We will begin by examining relationships of support
between reasons and conclusions, and go on to revise and extend an
understanding of flaws in the structure of the reasoning.

 EXAM TIP

> *In the exam you are likely to be asked to evaluate the support given by the reasoning
> to the author's main conclusion, or to a significant intermediate conclusion. You may
> be asked to make selective reference to flaws, assumptions, evidence and examples
> and to how well reasons support the conclusion. You will need to explain the impact
> of any strength or weakness on the support for the conclusion.*

How well do reasons support the conclusion?

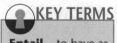 **KEY TERMS**

Entail – to have as
a necessary
consequence

You should be familiar with the idea that some reasons give better
support to a conclusion than others. One part of evaluating a longer
argument is deciding to what extent the author's main claims are
supported by their reasons.

 **KEY TERMS**

Valid – in a valid
argument, the
conclusion must be
true if the reasons
are true

Valid arguments

Some arguments have such a strong structure that, if the reasons are
true, the conclusion follows logically, and must also be true. That is,
the reasons **entail** the conclusion. These arguments have a **valid**
structure. They are known as deductive arguments, or deductively
valid.

For example:

> *Every member of the McCulloch family can play a musical instrument. Callum is a member of the McCulloch family. Therefore Callum must be able to play a musical instrument.*

This argument applies a general statement to a particular situation. It is valid because, if the reasons are true, the conclusion must also be true. The structure of this argument is:

R1   All As are B

R2   C is A

C   Therefore C is B.

It is possible to use diagrams to help us visualise the relationships between the general statements and the particular situation.

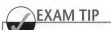

EXAM TIP

Don't panic if you prefer using words to symbols. You will not need to reduce an argument structure to this kind of notation, using A, B and C in the Critical Thinking exam. However, if your mind works in this logical way, symbols can be a useful tool to help you.

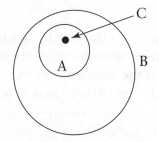 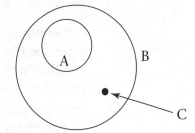

If C is in circle A, it is also in circle B. However, it is possible for C to be in circle B without being in circle A.

Let's take another example:

> *Every member of the McCulloch family can play a musical instrument. Morag cannot play a musical instrument. So Morag is not a member of the McCulloch family.*

This argument also applies a general idea to a specific case and has a valid structure:

R1   All As are B

R2   C is not B

C   Therefore C is not A.

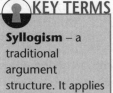

If we look at the diagram, we can see that if C is not in circle B, then it cannot be in circle A.

Both of these valid arguments are **syllogisms**.

Invalid arguments

Not all syllogisms have a valid structure. Just like other argument structures, some of them do not support their conclusion. Consider the following example:

> Every member of the McCulloch family can play a musical instrument. Katie can play a musical instrument. So Katie is a member of the McCulloch family.

This argument has an invalid structure:

All As are B

C is B

Therefore C is A.

It does not provide support for the conclusion, because there are lots of people who play musical instruments, not only the McCulloch family. If we look back at the diagram, we can see that C can be in circle B without being in circle A. Let's look at one more example:

> Every member of the McCulloch family can play a musical instrument. Owen is not a member of the McCulloch family. So Owen cannot play a musical instrument.

This argument also has an invalid structure. The structure here is:

R1   All As are B

R2   C is not A

C   Therefore C is not B.

So the argument fails to support the conclusion because it is possible for C to be in circle B without being in circle A. Lots of people play musical instruments, not just the McCulloch family.

Both of these invalid structures seem to be applying a general idea to a particular case, but the general idea does not relate to the particular case in a way that entails the conclusion.

ACTIVITY ⓴

a) Decide whether the following arguments have a valid structure.

A All students at Crumbleigh College are entitled to use the Learning Resource Centre (LRC). Sarah is a student at Crumbleigh College. So Sarah is entitled to use the LRC.

B All students at Crumbleigh College are entitled to use the Learning Resource Centre (LRC). Jamie is not a student at Crumbleigh College. So Jamie cannot be entitled to use the LRC.

b) Which one of the following arguments is valid?

A Everyone on Schooner Road has a boat. Jules has a boat. So Jules must live on Schooner Road.

B Everyone in the hockey team also plays water polo. Harrie is in the hockey team. So Harrie plays water polo.

C Elephants have trunks. Anda has a trunk. So Anda is an elephant.

D The only way to travel from Cotswa to Vend is by canoe. Indi has just left Cotswa by canoe. Indi must be travelling to Vend.

Applying your understanding of syllogisms to everyday arguments

Most arguments you will come across in everyday life will not be written as syllogisms, and they will not have conclusions which must be true. The really interesting issues are often those where the conclusion cannot be shown to be true. They tend to be inductive arguments, in which reasons give support to a conclusion and make the conclusion plausible, but do not mean that it must be true. So, when you are evaluating the support given to an author's conclusion, you will need to look for reasons which give us grounds to accept the conclusion, rather than expecting authors to show that their conclusion must be true. However, during their arguments authors will often apply a general idea to a particular situation. This may be a statement which is claimed to be generally true, or a recommendation, such as a principle, which applies generally. In these cases you can use your understanding of syllogisms to decide whether an author has used a valid argument structure to support their claims or not. Let's look at an extract from the article on happiness from Chapter 2:

> *Happiness has gone respectable, and it's been tagged to intellectual disciplines – the science of happiness, happiness economics – so it will be taken more seriously.*

This segment of the argument depends on an assumption that intellectual disciplines are taken seriously. We could re-write this argument in the form of a syllogism:

> R1   *Intellectual disciplines are taken seriously.*   (All As are B)
>
> R2   *Happiness is now an intellectual discipline.*   (C is A)
>
> C   *So, happiness will be taken more seriously.*   (Therefore C is B).

This does have a valid structure, so, if the reasons are true, the conclusion must be true. But there is an important difference between *being* an intellectual discipline, and *being tagged* to an intellectual discipline, so we cannot be certain that the conclusion is true. However, the form of the argument is sound, and we cannot say that the conclusion is totally unsupported.

You can also use the patterns of reasoning we have been looking at to help you sort through general ideas and specific information to decide what must, cannot or might be true.

ACTIVITY ㉑

> … Last year, every student who participated in Firmagh College's French exchange achieved a grade B or better.

Alice: 'Bas and I were lucky enough to attend evening cookery lessons with our exchange partners at the catering college in France. Our friend Leigh was even more disappointed that she couldn't come when we told her.'

French Results

Abiba Bas	A
Harris Siobhán	A
Page Blanche	C
Smith Jaya	E
Whyte Leigh	
Yardley Alice	

Which of the following statements must be true?

1) **Blanche did not go on the French exchange**

2) **Siobhán went on the French exchange.**

3) **Alice achieved either A or B in French.**

4) **Leigh achieved below grade B in French.**

   A 1 and 3

   B 1 only

   C 2, 3 and 4

   D 3 and 4

Do the reasons support the conclusion?

It is sometimes the case that an author has written a persuasive argument, but that the reasons do not support their precise conclusion. If we return to the happiness example, we can see that the author has used a valid argument structure, but she has implied that tagging happiness to intellectual disciplines is the same as making happiness an intellectual discipline. Sceptics may, however, dismiss it as a pseudo-science. So the author has not fully supported her strong conclusion that, 'happiness will be taken more seriously.' She has given us reason to consider that, 'happiness *is likely* to be taken more seriously by many people.'

EXAM TIP

Do make evaluative comments, such as 'The author has provided strong support for the intermediate conclusion, but the move to their main conclusion is ineffective because it depends on an unfounded assumption.' Support comments like this with reasons and explanations. Avoid working systematically through the argument listing reasons the author has used.

REMEMBER

Remember, an **assumption** is an unstated step which is essential to the argument.

We need to question the impact of this slight weakness on the author's main conclusion. In order to consider that, 'the state should resume a role in promoting the good life, not just chivvy us along in the global rat race, anxious and insecure,' we only need to accept that it is possible to take happiness seriously, not that it will be taken seriously. So the main conclusion stands.

When you are evaluating how well the author's reasons support the intermediate and main conclusions of an argument, you need to identify and comment on key points. Consider whether the reasons do give us grounds to accept the intermediate conclusions, and whether the intermediate conclusions do give us grounds to accept the main conclusion.

Assumptions

It may be that the reasons do not fully support a conclusion because the argument depends on unstated assumptions. In this case, we need to identify the assumptions precisely, and evaluate their impact on the argument. Assumptions may not be problematic. The assumption in the happiness article, that 'Intellectual disciplines are taken seriously' cannot easily be challenged, and it does form part of a valid argument structure.

However, some arguments rely on assumptions which can be challenged, or which are used in a weak argument structure. For example:

> *Dawn is a girl, so she'll be more interested in handbags and shoes than politics.*

This argument depends on the assumption that, 'Girls are more interested in handbags and shoes than politics.' The structure of the argument is valid:

Girls are more interested in shoes and handbags than politics.

Dawn is a girl.

So, Dawn must be more interested in shoes and handbags than politics.

If the reasons are true, the conclusion must be true. However, the assumption here is not just a general statement, but a generalisation.

It is too sweeping to say that ALL girls are more interested in shoes and handbags than politics. Because this argument depends on a sweeping generalisation, it does not support its conclusion.

ACTIVITY ㉒

Evaluate the support given in the following argument to the claim that 'the state sector should be reduced.'

Support your evaluation with selective reference to:

- assumptions which must be made and their impact on the reasoning
- how well the claim is supported by reasons and intermediate conclusions.

> This paper acknowledges that there are countless compassionate, conscientious people working selflessly in the public sector. Whether they are teachers, nurses or local authority workers, they are dedicated to producing a better society. We salute them. However, the state sector should be reduced.
>
> The state sector is inefficient, bloated, burdened by layer after layer of pointless bureaucracy and reaching into every nook and cranny of our national life. Since 1997, over 600,000 staff have been added to the public payroll, with 6.8 million adults – about one in four of the working population – now employed by the state.
>
> Yet Britain is now no better governed. A Home Office beyond satire ... the shambles over tax credits ... a multi-billion pound NHS computer that cost three times more than it should ... a Defra that can't get payments to farmers ... chaos at the Child Support Agency ... incompetence is everywhere.
>
> *Source*: **Daily Mail**, *7 June 2006*

Structural (or logical) flaws

As you learned at Critical Thinking AS Level, there are a number of flaws, or problems with a pattern of reasoning, which are easily recognisable as weakening the support for a conclusion. At AS Level you needed to be able to identify a flaw in the reasoning and to explain what was wrong with it. At A2 Level you also need to be able to assess *how far a flaw weakens an argument overall*.

You may find it useful to have another look at Chapter 5 in *Critical Thinking for OCR Unit 2* to remind yourself of some common flaws and explanations of what is wrong with them. In this chapter we will not cover every flaw in detail, but will concentrate on extending your skill in evaluating the impact of flawed reasoning on an argument. In Chapter 5, when we focus on rhetorical persuasion, we will consider how flaws such as appeals to popularity or authority can weaken the support for a claim.

Generalisation

As we have seen, general statements do have a role in argument structure. The process of forming general statements from observation of specific evidence is a fundamental part of science. Scientists watched the planets and formed the general rule that 'all planets orbit the sun.' To some extent all of us make sense of the world by generalising from the specific instances and examples in our lives. A baby watches people and learns that smiles are good.

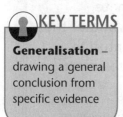

KEY TERMS

Generalisation – drawing a general conclusion from specific evidence

However, there are limits to this process of generalisation. A **generalisation** which is drawn from too little evidence is **hasty**, and does not support a conclusion. For example:

> *I have a handful of red sweets. So all sweets are red.*

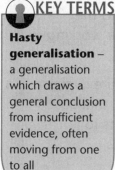

KEY TERMS

Hasty generalisation – a generalisation which draws a general conclusion from insufficient evidence, often moving from one to all

We can see immediately that this is a hasty generalisation, because our experience tells us that there are sweets of many colours. However, if we had only ever seen red sweets, we would not know this. In more complex situations, or situations where we have little personal experience, it is still possible to spot and question a hasty generalisation. For example:

> *Benzyl benzoate has been found to have unpleasant side effects, including irritating the skin. It is too dangerous to use chemicals in shampoos and cosmetics.*

This argument depends on the assumptions that, 'unpleasant side effects are dangerous' and 'all chemicals have unpleasant side effects.' Both are generalisations. One chemical used in shampoo which might give some people itchy skin is not enough evidence to show that all chemicals are too dangerous to use. We only need one example to demonstrate that some chemicals are safe. One example is enough to show that a very strong, or general claim isn't the case. For example:

> H_2O is a chemical which does not have dangerous or unpleasant side effects when used in cosmetics.

This one example weakens the very strong, general claim that, 'all chemicals have unpleasant side effects.' It does not show that it is safe to use any chemical in cosmetics. So, when you are evaluating the impact of a generalisation on an author's reasoning, you may say that the one example given does not entail the general conclusion drawn. This does not mean that the conclusion is wrong; just that it is not supported by the reasoning given.

One counter example causes a problem for a general rule. So, a **sweeping generalisation**, (for example, girls are more interested in shoes than politics) tends to weaken the support for a claim. We cannot be sure that Dawn is more interested in shoes than politics. Even though many girls are more interested in shoes than politics, there are exceptions to this generalisation, and we cannot be sure that Dawn is not an exception.

This kind of stereotyping generalisation is commonly found in the media, and informs prejudice, abuse, bullying and even government policy. It can be annoying, hurtful and even cruel. However, such sweeping generalisation is poor reasoning and fails to support its conclusion. So we should be aware of it in everyday life as well as in Critical Thinking exams.

In a short argument, a flaw such as a hasty or sweeping generalisation does mean that we do not have to accept the conclusion. In a longer argument, a flaw may weaken the support but not totally destroy it. Where there are two or more strands of reasoning, if one is flawed, the other may still provide some support.

Flaw of causation

In everyday life and science we also think about causal relationships. The baby smiles, and receives love and attention. It is not unreasonable for the baby to think that the smiles cause the love and attention. It is certainly a useful rule of thumb that people react better to us if we smile at them. However, it is problematic to assume

REMEMBER

Remember, **entail** means have as a necessary consequence. So one example does not entail a general rule. But one counter example does entail a problem with a general rule.

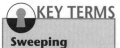

KEY TERMS

Sweeping generalisation – a generalisation that moves from many to all, creating a stereotype

KEY TERMS

Flaw of causation – a flaw in reasoning which assumes that if two things happen at the same time or one after the other, one of them must have caused the other. However, this is not enough to infer a causal link

that if two things are correlated, and happen at the same time or one after the other, that one causes the other.

In the baby's case, it is probably not the smile which causes the love. The love probably exists anyway. The smile probably provides a spark for the attention, and encourages the parent to show their love. But it is probably not the only cause of the attention. The parent's love and desire to be a good parent may cause them to continue paying attention to the baby. The smiles help. There will also be occasions when smiling is not effective because no one is looking, or the parent is grumpy and tired. So, when we evaluate the baby's reasoning, we can say that it is flawed, and it oversimplifies the causal relationships. Yet we cannot say that the baby's conclusion is totally unsupported or unacceptable, and we certainly would not recommend the baby to stop smiling.

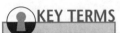

KEY TERMS

Inconsistency – parts of the argument which pull in different directions, or which would support different conclusions; often both cannot be true at the same time

Inconsistency

At Critical Thinking A2 Level you will be expected to recognise reasoning which contains **inconsistency,** and to evaluate the impact of this inconsistency on the overall argument. The inconsistency may be two pieces of evidence which would support different conclusions, or reasons which cannot both be true at the same time.

For example:

'Since the British Library recently opened its facilities to undergraduates, it has become difficult to find a seat unless you arrive soon after opening time,' complained one leading research historian. 'You only need to look at undergraduate reading lists to see that they don't need the facilities of a specialist research library. The library authorities should limit undergraduates' admission to the afternoons only, leaving the mornings free for serious scholars. That should not be a hardship, since undergraduates notoriously don't get up until midday anyway.'

In this example, it is inconsistent to claim both that undergraduates take all the seats in the morning and that they don't get up until midday. We need to ask whether this weakness is enough to take away all support for the conclusion.

If we ignore the last sentence, we can see that there are still two reasons to support the conclusion:

R1   Since the British Library opened its facilities to undergraduates, it has become difficult to find a seat unless you arrive soon after opening time.

R2   Undergraduates don't need the facilities of a specialist research library.

C   So the library authorities should limit undergraduates' admission to the afternoon.

So, we can take the inconsistency away and leave an argument that provides some support for the conclusion. The inconsistency exists between R1 and a further reason which is a throwaway comment, a sweeping generalisation which is not essential to the argument.

However, we can still not say that the conclusion is well supported. It depends on two assumptions.

1)   Undergraduates only need books on their reading lists.

2)   Undergraduates are not serious scholars.

Both of these assumptions can be challenged. Undergraduates may well need to research beyond the bare minimum on their reading lists, and some of them may be – or become – serious scholars. So the historian has not given good support for their conclusion.

ACTIVITY ㉓

Evaluate the support given by the reasoning in the following passages to the main conclusion. Support your evaluation by making selective reference to flaws in the reasoning and their impact on the strength of the reasoning.

a) The Divorce Reform Act, which made it easier for couples to obtain a divorce, came into effect in 1971. The annual rate of divorce has risen steadily since 1971. This law has led directly to family breakdown.

b) Fairness appears to be an instinctive trait common to primates. Researchers taught capuchin monkeys to trade small rocks for food rewards, serving two monkeys side by side so that each could see the trades offered the other. At first, the experimenters always gave the monkeys cucumber for their rocks. Then they began giving one monkey a grape, which capuchins prefer to cucumber. The other monkeys then often refused to trade. In another experiment, monkeys cooperated to pull a heavy bar to reveal food. A monkey who had eaten her portion of the food would return to help a second monkey get hers.

c) Global warming is a scam with no foundation in fact, perpetrated by dishonest, incompetent scientists with vested interests and no understanding of logic. The only evidence that human activity causes climate change is that temperature has increased since Western industrialisation. There is a closer correlation between this latest warming and everyone getting the vote. In science, the fact that events coincide does not mean that there is a causal link between them.

d) Our house went on the market on Wednesday 1 March. The estate agents didn't put a for sale sign up until Wednesday 8 March. It also took a week to get the house advertised on their 'You Should Move' website. When I phoned the estate agents, they said it was a problem with the website, but they had sent all the details on Friday 3 March. When the details came up on the website, there was a for sale sign in the picture of the house. The estate agent was not telling the truth.

ACTIVITY 24

Evaluate the support given by the reasoning in the following passages to the main conclusion. Support your evaluation by making selective reference to:

- flaws in the reasoning and their impact on the strength of the reasoning

- assumptions which must be made and their impact on the reasoning

- how well the claim is supported by reasons and intermediate conclusions.

> **!REMEMBER**
>
> Remember to look back at the list of flaws in *Critical Thinking for OCR Unit 2*. You may need to evaluate any of the flaws which appear in that list. In this chapter you have looked at how a small number of flaws affect the strength of an argument.

a) A woman who conceives as a result of contraceptive failure has not voluntarily undertaken a duty towards the foetus. So she cannot be held to have a duty towards the foetus, since she did all she could to avoid becoming pregnant. It would be quite unreasonable to tell women that they must live like nuns unless they are willing to run the risk of carrying a pregnancy to term, giving birth and then either caring for an uninvited member of the family for the next 18 years or suffering the mental anguish of giving a child up for adoption.

b) We should take no notice of those extreme liberals who want to ensure that terrorists receive a fair trial. What about the rights of those who are killed or maimed while going about their lawful business? Terrorists do not care about the rights of their victims. So we should not care about their right to a fair trial.

SUMMARY

You should now be able to evaluate the impact on the support for a conclusion of:

- reasons which give weak support to a conclusion

- unstated assumptions

- flaws in the reasoning.

Evaluating support for a claim: rhetorical persuasion

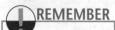
REMEMBER

Rhetorical persuasion uses emotional means to persuade an audience to accept an opinion, rather than giving reasons to support a conclusion.

In Chapter 1 we distinguished between argument, which gives reasons to support a conclusion, and rhetorical persuasion, which persuades you through clever use of words and emotive language rather than by giving good reasons to support a conclusion. In this chapter we will look at emotional and linguistic attempts to persuade, and the effect they can have on an argument.

Some of the flaws we considered at Critical Thinking AS Level are, strictly speaking, rhetorical moves which attempt to persuade emotionally. They offer little rational support for a conclusion, but are not structurally weak in the way that a hasty generalisation is weak. These 'rhetorical flaws', which we will consider in this chapter, include:

- appeals (to popularity, tradition, history and authority)
- attacking the arguer
- straw person
- slippery slope.

Appeals

REMEMBER

You can remind yourself about appeals to popularity, traditions, history and authority by looking at *Critical Thinking for OCR Unit 2*, Chapter 5.

You are familiar with appeals to popularity, tradition, history and authority. Other appeals include but are not limited to, appeals to fear, vanity, self-interest and novelty. They tend to play on our feelings, such as our fear of change, or desire to do what is best for ourselves.

An appeal to fear or an appeal to your self-interest or vanity might persuade you to agree to something. However, if you look more closely, you might see that there is no good reason given to support the conclusion. For example:

> *Any intelligent person can see that murderers should never be released from prison.*

Here, the writer is appealing to vanity, trying to persuade readers to accept their opinion by playing on their desire not to look stupid. The writer has not addressed any reasons why murderers should, or should not, be kept in prison for their natural lives.

ACTIVITY 25

a) Consider reasons for and against keeping murderers in prison until they die.

b) Consider what sort of evidence you might need to support these reasons.

c) Write two arguments to support or challenge the conclusion that murderers should remain in prison until they die. Make one argument as strong as you can, using evidence and reasons. In the other argument, use as many appeals as possible, and target your audience's emotions.

Are appeals always weaknesses?

Appeals are not necessarily flaws which weaken the support for a conclusion. This is partly because they are not trying to strengthen the rational support for a conclusion. A strong argument which gives good reasons to keep murderers in prison would not become weaker because it also included an appeal to popularity, for example. On its own, however, an appeal does not usually give us a reason to accept a conclusion, as we can see in the example:

> *Hundreds of thousands of people read their horoscopes in newspapers or magazines. So there must be some truth in them.*

Just because horoscope reading is popular, does not mean that horoscopes are right. This appeal to popularity totally fails to support the conclusion. Because it is the only reasoning offered, the conclusion is unsupported. However, there are times when an appeal can contribute to the support for a conclusion. For example:

> *Thousands of people read their horoscope in newspapers and magazines. So we should include horoscopes in our magazine.*

In this case, the popularity of horoscopes probably is a good reason to include them in a magazine, because including popular features sells magazines. If there were a good reason not to include horoscopes, this should probably override their popularity. Let's look at another example:

> *Most experts agree that the MMR vaccine is not dangerous. The one expert who disagrees has been found to have a vested interest, and has been discredited. Your child is considerably more likely to get a serious illness such as measles without the jab, even if single jabs are used instead of the combined MMR vaccine. So we should probably allow our children to be vaccinated with the MMR vaccine.*

In this case, the appeal to authority is reasonable. Although we could not conclude that we should definitely allow our children to be vaccinated on the basis of this appeal to authority, we should have a very good reason to reject the authority of experts. A fear that a vaccination might be dangerous should not outweigh expert opinion that lack of vaccination is more dangerous.

Let's look at another example:

> *We have always smoked in the office. We don't need some nanny state interfering in our lives. We should be able to carry on smoking in the office.*

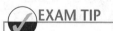

EXAM TIP

At Critical Thinking A2 Level, if you choose to comment on an appeal as part of your evaluation of an argument, you should consider how reasonable the appeal is, and whether it forms part of a strong argument, or is the only attempt to support a claim.

Just because we have always smoked in the office doesn't mean that it is the right thing to do. There are good reasons not to smoke in offices – it is bad for everyone's health, smelly and unappealing. So the appeal to tradition does not support the conclusion.

However, we might want to take tradition into account in an argument. There may be good reasons to prefer something which has stood the test of time to something new and untried. Furthermore, people often have emotional attachments to old, familiar things. This sort of emotional, subjective reason can be taken into consideration. It does not necessarily outweigh other considerations, but an appeal to tradition is not *necessarily* a weakness.

ACTIVITY 26

Evaluate the use of appeals in the following arguments.

a)

> It is currently illegal to strike in support of workers from other companies. But many small companies are dominated by large corporations which effectively dictate their working practices. More than 200 years ago, economist Adam Smith, examining strike action, concluded: 'The master can hold out much longer than the men ... In the long run, the workmen may be as necessary to the master, as the master is to them. But the necessity is not so imminent.' Trade unions were created to redress the balance. They cannot do that if they are prohibited from confronting the big companies that manipulate the small. So, it ought to be legal to withdraw labour from large companies closely associated with smaller firms in dispute with their employees.
>
> *Source: Adapted from an article by Roy Hattersley,* **The Guardian**, 19 September, *2005*

b)

> Tony Blair was wrong to abolish the office of Lord Chancellor in 2003. Britain has had Lord Chancellors for hundreds of years, and the position has helped to ensure the stability and fairness of our judicial system during that time. There are those who argue that it has been inefficient to have one minister combining the roles of Speaker of the House of Lords, Minister for Constitutional Affairs and Head of the Judiciary (appointing judges and overseeing their work). They have also suggested that this position of Lord Chancellor has contravened the principle of separation of political and legal powers. However, such a radical break with tradition should not have been announced suddenly without wide consultation and debate.

ACTIVITY 27

Evaluate the use of appeals in the article entitled 'Who says nuclear power is clean?' in Chapter 2 on pages 20–21.

Attacking and misrepresenting the opposition

Attacking the arguer rather than the argument, and misrepresenting the opposition's arguments (the straw person flaw) are also rhetorical moves rather than structural problems in the reasoning. Unlike appeals, which are not necessarily weak, it is generally a weakness in an argument to attack or misrepresent your opposition. Your own argument may well seem more persuasive if you have shown that your opponent is idiotic, or is using weak arguments. However, the argument will not become rationally stronger, and in Critical Thinking, we are concerned with arguments that persuade us with good, strong reasons.

When arguing that secondary action should be legal, the author began his argument:

> *Some phrases provoke emotion that is out of all proportion to their meaning. One of them is secondary picketing, an activity generally regarded as so obviously reprehensible that trade unionists who argue for its legalisation are regarded as clinically insane. The establishment has always dismissed, as not worth discussing, conduct that threatens its position but can be justified on merit. Mindless disapproval is more convenient than thought. Secondary picketing – indeed, secondary action in general – is, on any rational analysis, often justified and frequently laudable.*
>
> Source: Adapted from an article by Roy Hattersley, **The Guardian**, 19 September, 2005

Here, the author uses a straw person flaw, accusing the opposition of mindless disapproval and emotional responses. This probably misrepresents the arguments of many of those who oppose secondary action – many of whom probably believe that secondary action is economically damaging, and hurts those who are on strike more than the companies they work for. The author also accuses the opposition of flawed reasoning (dismissing secondary action as not worth discussion), which may be unfair. These moves are both used to convince the reader that the arguments which have seemed so strong are in fact quite weak. This feeling is reinforced by the appeal in the last line, which manipulates the reader into feeling that any opposition not only is not, but cannot be, rational.

However, because he has to a certain extent misrepresented opposing arguments, the author has not answered counter arguments, or given us reason to accept his view rather than any other. There is enough truth in the author's version of his opponents' arguments to make the audience consider whether their own objection might be based on emotion rather than reason; this argument defuses hostility to secondary action, rather than responding to argument with argument. It is also more amusing this way, and people who read papers do want to be entertained as well as provoked into thought.

Slippery slopes

At Critical Thinking AS Level we defined a slippery slope flaw as reasoning which moves from one minor event through a series of unconnected events to an extreme consequence. There are many examples of such extreme slippery slopes to be found. However, there are also more subtle versions, where the events are connected, and the extreme consequence does not seem so unlikely. For example:

> *Once a man is permitted on his own authority to kill an innocent person directly, there … are no longer any rational grounds for saying that [killing others] can advance so far and no further. Once the exception has been made it is too late. Euthanasia under any circumstances must be condemned.*
>
> *Once the respect for human life is so low that an innocent person may be killed directly at his own request, compulsory euthanasia will necessarily be very near. This could lead easily to killing all incurable cancer patients, the aged who are in public care, wounded soldiers, all deformed children, the mentally afflicted, and so on. Before long the danger would be at the door of every citizen.*
>
> Source: Bishop Joseph Sullivan, 'The immorality of euthanasia,' in The Morality of
> Mercy Killing, *Westminster Md: Newman Press, 1950*

It does seem that there is a psychological barrier to killing innocent people. Once we have broken down that barrier, it is hard to know how we would prevent the category of people who can be killed from being extended to those who have not given their consent. It is easy to imagine a government which refuses health treatment to the obese, to smokers or to drinkers because they have not looked after themselves, deciding that those with specific illnesses cost the state too much money, and should be assisted in an early, painless and non-voluntary death. It is easy to imagine relatives who are happy to ease Granny out of her misery when she is not able to speak for herself, especially if Granny is both rich and irritating. This is a good reason for keeping that psychological barrier intact.

On the other hand, there may be ways of exploring logical differences between exceptions to the principle that we should not kill innocent people. It may not be a necessary consequence of allowing voluntary euthanasia. There is also a big step between compulsory euthanasia of the old, ill and deformed and the danger being at the door of every citizen. It is not an impossible step, especially in a society as obsessed with physical beauty and body image as ours. But it is still a big step.

ACTIVITY 28

The issue of euthanasia has been debated in Parliament again in 2005–6. Research the arguments that are used for and against euthanasia. Have any of them successfully answered the concern that allowing voluntary euthanasia may be the first step on a slippery slope?

Language

In Critical Thinking we are concerned with language only to the extent that it communicates ideas or support for a conclusion. Because language is the tool for communicating our thinking, poor or confused use of language can seriously weaken the support for a conclusion.

Emotion

Language which makes us emotional is often used instead of clear, precise language which expresses reasons to support conclusions. Let's look at two ways of putting the same point:

> A   *It's time our fine, hardworking nurses got the recognition they deserve. These saints of our society slave away night and day, toiling for the benefit of us all.*

> B   *Nurses are hard working, dedicated professionals who provide care to those in need. We should recognise this and reward them appropriately. Nurses' pay should be increased to take into account the professional training, the long, hard hours, the disruption of shift work, and the importance of the services they provide.*

Passage A uses emotional language to persuade us. Nurses are described in glowing terms, making us feel that they deserve more. However, it is barely an argument, and could be knocked down very easily.

Passage B is more factual, and clearly gives reasons to support the conclusion in the last sentence. It requires the reader to work a little harder – and it is harder to use your reason than it is to respond emotionally. It is, however, worth it in the long run if it helps you to make better decisions. For example, we would certainly want to make decisions about issues such as people's pay, or who to vote for, on the basis of reason rather than fear or vanity.

KEY TERMS

conflation – bringing different concepts together and treating them as the same

Conflation and equivocation

As you learned at Critical Thinking AS Level, **conflation** is bringing two or more different concepts together and treating them as the same. For example, in the passage on happiness in Chapter 2 on pages 23–24, the author treats unhappiness and mental ill health as the same. This weakens her argument because there are clear differences.

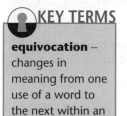

KEY TERMS

equivocation – changes in meaning from one use of a word to the next within an argument

Equivocation is the use of a single word with different meanings in the same argument. For example:

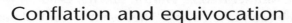

> *It is generally recognised that being able to choose whether or not to have a child is a universal right. This is why many countries have criticised the Chinese government's policy of only allowing couples to have one child. Couples in the UK who are unable to have children naturally are being deprived of this universal right of procreative choice unless they can afford expensive medical procedures. So the British government's failure to allow these procedures on the NHS is a breach of this universal right.*

In this case, there is an equivocation, with the first 'universal right' meaning a freedom to do something and the other two references to 'universal right' meaning a right to receive something. There is also a conflation between choosing how to use your natural abilities, and a right to treatment to overcome natural problems with reproduction.

ACTIVITY 29

Evaluate the reasoning in the following passage. Support your evaluation with selective reference to:

- any flaws in the reasoning and their impact on the overall reasoning

- any rhetorical attempts to persuade and their impact on the overall reasoning.

A packed lunch raid has left children in tears after their crisps and biscuits have been confiscated. The school says it has repeatedly asked parents not to send their children to school with crisps and chocolate in order to improve the learning environment. Step-dad Sean puts his arm around 8 year-old Shawna and says, 'I don't like the way they've done it, Shawna was upset. But it's like that Jamie Oliver said, kids have got to have good food if they're going to be healthy and do the best they can in life.' Most parents, however, are up in arms, claiming that teachers should not tell them what their children should eat. Mother Debbie Warton said her children were terribly upset at having their food taken away. 'They want to control our lives. I give my girls a balanced lunch. They go dancing and they're not fat. The teacher's taken half their lunch away and not replaced it with anything.' Dad Kieran May adds, 'My boy would've had sausages and chips in the canteen. Seems like it's all right for the school to provide junk dinners, but it's not all right to have crisps in your packed lunch. Doesn't make sense.' Grandad Zafar Iqbal said his granddaughter Charlene had been in tears. 'The school and the government want to tell us what's best. Where is it going to end? Are they going to tell us what to eat at home?'

ACTIVITY 30

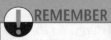
REMEMBER

Remember that you will gain credit for identifying strength as well as weakness.

Evaluate the reasoning in the following passage. Support your evaluation with selective reference to:

- any flaws in the reasoning and their impact on the overall reasoning

- any rhetorical attempts to persuade and their impact on the overall reasoning

Selfish, smug, self-righteous, unbearable two-wheeled idiots!

1 Cyclists are a danger to us all. They're aggressive, foulmouthed oafs, a far cry from the virtuous saints they'd have us believe they are. Once cyclists symbolised the slow, gentle pace of genteel rural life. Now they are a menace to the public and should not be allowed on our roads.

2 Gentility and modesty have been replaced with arrogance and aggression. Brimming with hostility, utterly indifferent to those around them, they appear to think they're above the law. As if laws about red lights, pavements or one-way streets applied to them! These lycra monsters ooze contempt for pedestrians and motorists, and have made travel around London a nightmare.

3 Worse, they behave as if they were somehow morally superior to the rest of us. They flaunt their politically correct badge of greenness as if it allowed them total freedom of action. Swear at motorists? Why not! Bowl pedestrians over? Abuse them for getting in the way! A green outlook is supposed to be based on a concern for your surroundings, but cyclists routinely abuse their surroundings.

4 This is all the more infuriating, as their environmentalism is, in any case, mostly posturing. Half of them have a car driving behind them with their briefcase; most of them jet off for trendy weekend breaks, oozing smugness as their planes belch noxious gases into the clouds. They do not question whether their ghastly lycra was made by exploited 6 year-olds in Third World countries, or whether their trendy bicycle was manufactured in a low-wage factory in China.

5 These people don't even pay road taxes – they get to use the roads we pay for without contributing a penny, yet they abuse us for the privilege. These people should be made to pay, and they should be licensed and they should be punished if they do not abide by the regulations of the road.

6 Cyclists make us law abiding citizens foam at the mouth and dream of slashing their tyres and jamming sticks in their spokes to bring them down to earth and the realities of motoring. We need a return to a gentler era, when cyclists were well mannered, and young men were routinely locked up for cycling without lights. Then it might become clear that moral superiority does not come from owning a bicycle.

SUMMARY

You should now be able to:

- identify rhetorical attempts to persuade

- evaluate the impact of rhetorical persuasion on a piece of reasoning.

Evaluating reasoning: counter argument, hypothetical reasoning and analogy

In this chapter we will consider how to evaluate patterns of reasoning which are not covered by structural, logical flaws (Chapter 4) or problems of language and rhetoric (Chapter 5). We will examine counter argument, hypothetical reasoning and analogies.

EXAM TIP

These patterns of reasoning are often a good source of evaluative comments about the strength of an argument. In Unit 4 Section B you will access good marks if you show a clear understanding of weakness in argument by looking at the impact of flaws on the reasoning. You will access the highest marks if you are also able to show a clear and accurate understanding of strength *in an argument.*

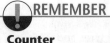

REMEMBER

Counter argument (CA) is an opposing argument which is shown to be wrong in order to strengthen the author's argument.

Counter argument

An argument is essentially one sided – it provides reasons to support a conclusion. However, it may be important to deal with opposing views or anticipated counter arguments as part of an argument. If opposing views can be effectively dealt with, the support for a conclusion should be stronger. You should already be familiar with short counter arguments from your Critical Thinking AS Level studies. For example:

> While **some may argue that we should cull poultry in Scotland because a swan has died of bird flu**, this view is an overreaction. A single death is not yet an epidemic. Nor can bird flu be transmitted from human to human. A wholesale cull of birds would have consequences far worse than the virus itself. More measured precautions should be taken to prevent the spread of bird flu.

If we analyse this short argument, we find that the first sentence is a counter argument, consisting of a reason and a conclusion:

CA   R   *a swan has died of bird flu*

         C   *we should cull all the birds in Scotland.*

The main conclusion, at the end, is that more measured precautions should be taken to prevent the spread of bird flu.

Identifying counter argument

In the multiple choice section of the paper, you may come across questions which ask for the best expression of the counter argument in the passage, or which ask what function an element has and include a counter argument in the answers.

ACTIVITY 31

Most body parts grow in proportion with each other as individuals of a species become larger, but male sexual traits that are attractive to females, such as antlers or a peacock's feathery display, become disproportionately large as body size increases. In a study of 284 ornament-bearing species it was found that the ornament grew by roughly the square of the overall growth rate. This may seem a waste of energy and resources, but extra-large ornaments are more effective at attracting females than a slightly larger body.

Source: New Scientist, *27 May 2006 p.21*

Which of the following best expresses the counter argument in the passage?

A Almost all parts of the body grow in proportion with each other as an individual grows.

B Male sexual traits become disproportionately large as body size increases.

C Growing large ornaments appears to be a waste of resources.

D Extra large ornaments are more effective at attracting females than a larger body.

Suggesting effective counter argument

Identifying the best expression of a counter argument would be an analytic task. A more complex question might present you with four options, and ask you which would most effectively counter the argument. This would begin to use your evaluative skills because you would be making a judgement.

ACTIVITY 32

Prescription drug abuse is out of control in the US. Users are visiting websites in their millions to find out how to tamper with medicines which contain drugs such as opioids to make it possible to eat, inject or smoke them. The only way to find out if these methods are safe is to try them. However, all these drugs are lethal or toxic in high enough doses, so trying could be fatal. There are ways of making drugs tamper proof. Although it is expensive, drug companies can, for example, make tablets harder, use foul-tasting ingredients or add a substance that blocks psychoactive hits. Pharmaceutical companies must do as much as they can to make their medicines tamper proof.

a) Which of the following best expresses the counter argument in the passage?

A Many people are tampering with prescription drugs to get high.

B Prescription drugs can poison or kill people if enough of them are taken.

C Making drugs tamper proof is expensive.

D Pharmaceutical companies are not interested in making their medicines safe.

b) Which of the following would most effectively counter the argument in the passage?

A People will always find a way to tamper with drugs, whatever pharmaceutical companies do to stop them.

B Making medicines tamper proof would make them less effective for patients.

C There should be stricter controls over who can get hold of prescription drugs.

D If people cannot get legal drugs, they will buy illegal drugs.

Use of counter argument

Presenting a counter argument is different from presenting a balanced view of an issue. There is no intention to weigh up the merits of different views. A counter argument is there to be rejected, and thus strengthen the author's own reasoning/conclusion. Sometimes this process will involve presenting a sustained counter argument, which shows more of the reasoning supporting the counter conclusion. This provides more opportunities to show that this reasoning is flawed or inadequate, and thus weakens the counter argument.

There are four main stages to this process:

1) State the counter claims

2) Examine the support given to them

3) Show that this support is not strong

4) Provide alternative reasoning.

An author does not need to do all of these, but may well do so in a piece of sustained counter argument. Let's work through these steps with the example we used earlier.

State the counter claim

'We should cull poultry in Scotland because a swan has died of bird flu.'

Examine the support given to this claim

An author might choose to show that the reasons supporting the conclusion are inadequate. But first, the author must show what those reasons might be.

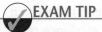

EXAM TIP

A counter argument is a perfect opportunity for a straw person flaw. Although not every counter argument is flawed in this way, look out for exaggerations and distortions of the opposing argument, which make it easier to reject a counter argument.

> *Bird flu is a highly contagious virus which spreads from wild birds to domestic poultry. Humans have caught bird flu from infected birds. The Scottish swan probably infected other birds, which might infect domestic poultry. If domestic poultry becomes infected, the chance of bird-to-human transmission of the virus increases. The more people get the disease, the more chance there is, not only of human deaths, but of the virus mutating so that it can move between humans. If this deadly virus developed the ability to move between humans, there would be a lethal epidemic. We wish to avoid an epidemic, so we should cull domestic poultry to prevent it happening.*

Show that this support is not strong

The depicted chain of events is perfectly possible. We cannot seriously disagree that we wish to avoid an epidemic, and any government which did not take suitable preventative measures would be in breach of its duty of care towards the population. However, there are a number of ways in which we could show this argument to be inadequate, or too weak to support its conclusion:

- Probability
- Choice of moment for intervention
- Choice of action
- Ignores other options.

Probability The chain of events is possible, but not necessarily probable. Domestic poultry will not necessarily become infected, nor will people in this country necessarily catch the virus (due to British Health and Safety regulations), nor will the virus necessarily mutate so that it can move between humans.

On the other hand, culling domestic poultry will not necessarily prevent an epidemic. If the virus spreads between wild birds, and humans interact with those birds (by wiping faeces off cars or hair or whatever), it remains possible that a human version of the virus could develop. It would be less likely, but nevertheless possible.

Choice of moment for intervention One wild bird has been found to have a virus. Is this the right moment for intervention by culling domestic fowl? Although we want to act in time to prevent an epidemic, it seems sensible to wait until there is strong evidence of a problem rather than rushing in with drastic measures.

Choice of action   Culling all domestic fowl seems a drastic measure, especially if the possibility of transmission of the virus between chickens and humans is minimal, and culling them will still leave a significant risk of infection from wild birds. This measure would do a lot of damage in terms of lives lost, livelihoods lost and panic and demoralisation of communities.

Ignores other options The argument restricts the options by ignoring other measures which could be taken to prevent an epidemic.

EXAM TIP

It is sometimes tempting to put a great deal of thought into giving reasons why an opponent's view is weak, and too little effort into providing a strong argument to support your own view. Many arguments in daily life suffer from this weakness. In the exam you would not access the highest marks if you gave too little support to your own conclusion.

Provide alternative reasoning

Alternative reasoning might consist of support in this case for alternative measures, such as vaccination, increased health and safety measures for workers dealing with poultry, public awareness campaigns, flu masks, and so on.

Consideration of a number of different counter claims

Rather than looking in detail at one counter argument, an author might try to dismiss a number of counter claims before providing their own reasoning to support their own claims. If you are arguing against a popularly held belief, this may be necessary. In an argument of the length that can be found in the press, however, this may lead to an author dismissing counter arguments in a hurried, flawed or rhetorical manner. To do so properly might take more words than are available.

If an author dismisses a number of claims, look for straw person flaws, attacks on the arguer or dismissal without sufficient grounds. For example:

> *University education should be available only to the academic elite. Some may argue that education is a right for all, but these are largely unintelligent, ignorant young people clamouring about their rights to everything and their responsibilities to no one. Education is vital to the economy, they cry, but a detailed knowledge of medieval German poetry is of no use to anyone. Others claim that education expands the soul, but I have seen no evidence of this. On the contrary, university education is expensive, and suitable only for an academic elite who are in any case unfitted for economic productivity.*

In this argument, the author attacks the arguer rather than the argument, calling those who argue for education for all unintelligent and ignorant, but not addressing their reasoning. The assertion that they are clamouring for rights without responsibility misrepresents the arguments of people who wish for education for all, and is a straw person flaw. It is unreasonable to dismiss the counter argument that education is vital to the economy with a narrow example such as medieval German poetry, because there is clearly more to education than this. The response to the counter argument about education expanding the soul is inadequate; just because the author has seen no evidence of this does not make it wrong.

Let's examine the article on nuclear power, which is found in Chapter 2 on pages 20–21, concentrating on the author's use of counter argument.

The bulk of this article consists of a detailed rejection of three counter claims that nuclear power is clean, reliable and secure. These claims are, as we discussed in Chapter 3, challenged by strong evidence. The author's own case, that we should consider alternative, renewable energy sources more seriously, is less well developed. In fairness to the author, this may have been because of limited space dictated by the newspaper. All the same, a strong rejection of claims for nuclear

ACTIVITY 33

Read the article on happiness, which is found in Chapter 2 on pages 23–24.

a) The first three paragraphs respond to an unstated counter claim. What is this assumed counter claim?

b) Evaluate the use and rejection of the counter argument, 'The emotional life of citizens is no business of the state...'

c) Evaluate the use and dismissal of the counter argument, 'To some, these kinds of interventions represent a nightmare scenario of a nanny state, an unacceptable interference in personal freedom. If people want to pursue their own unhappiness, then the state has no right to stop them.'

power does not in itself make a strong case for renewable power.

We will return to counter arguments in Chapter 7, looking at how you may use them in your own arguments.

Hypothetical reasoning

Hypothetical reasoning uses an 'if ... then' claim to support a conclusion. In a longer passage this may be an intermediate conclusion. As we saw in *Critical Thinking for OCR Unit 2*, we have to consider three issues/questions:

- Is the hypothetical claim as a whole likely?
- Is the hypothetical event likely?

- Are the hypothetical consequences likely?

A further consideration at A2 Critical Thinking concerns the impact of the hypothetical reasoning on the author's argument as a whole:

- Is the reasoning unlikely or extreme?
- Does the hypothetical reasoning provide support for the author's overall reasoning?

> *If the bird flu virus mutates so that it can be transmitted from human to human, there will be a terrible epidemic costing thousands, if not millions of lives.*

So in this case we have to consider how likely it is that the bird flu virus will mutate. Scientific opinion at the time of writing indicates that it is possible, but not probable. An important part of considering the likeliness of a claim is often identifying the evidence needed to verify a claim and evaluating this evidence.

The hypothetical consequence, that there would be a terrible epidemic, seems fairly likely, as the virus is spreading rapidly and fatally through the world's avian population, and has already killed humans. It is difficult to verify a hypothetical claim such as this. But by considering how likely its parts are, we can reach a view about the claim as a whole. The hypothetical claim about a bird flu epidemic seems likely enough to be worth taking seriously. This is backed up by the gravity of the hypothetical consequences.

In this case, then, we accept the hypothetical reasoning. However, as we discussed earlier, there were a number of reasons why this did not provide good support for the main conclusion, that we should cull domestic poultry to prevent an epidemic.

Philosophers sometimes use unlikely hypothetical consequences to help them establish a principle. For example, if you could know with certainty that your next door neighbour's child was going to become a brutal dictator, you may have to think long and hard about whether it would be more wrong to kill the child, or to let it live and kill many others. In everyday life, however, we cannot work with such unlikely extremes.

ACTIVITY ③④

Consider the following arguments which contain hypothetical reasoning. Evaluate the likeliness of the hypothetical claims and the support they provide for the main conclusion.

a) If I shout at my friend for eating too much chocolate, she will feel bad. So she will stop eating chocolate.

b) Wi-Fi wine glasses which glow when your loved one is drinking have been developed. If couples in long-distance relationships use such glasses, they will feel as if they are having a shared experience. If they are having shared experiences, couples are less likely to become emotionally distant. If they do not become emotionally distant, they are less likely to split up.

c) If we allow genetic engineering of babies, people in 1000 years' time will be more intelligent, healthy, beautiful and emotionally stable. This would be a positive consequence, so we should promote the legalisation of human genetic engineering.

🔑 KEY TERMS

Sustained hypothetical reasoning – reasoning in which an author looks at a chain of 'ifs' and their consequences, or a long look at the consequences of one 'if'

Sustained hypothetical reasoning

In a longer passage, you may come across **sustained hypothetical reasoning**. This can take the form of:

- a chain of 'ifs', such as Activity 34b) above
- one 'if', followed by a sustained look at the consequences.

A chain of 'ifs' may be complex, subtle and very interesting. On the other hand, like any chain of reasoning, it is vulnerable, because if one link does not hold, neither does the conclusion. This kind of reasoning is also inclined to become a slippery slope. It need not, but may.

A single hypothetical claim might lead to a sustained examination of possible consequences. Let's take an excerpt from the article on happiness in Chapter 2 on page 23:

> *It raises the prospect of a future politics where emotional wellbeing could be as important a remit of state public health policy as our physical wellbeing. In 10 years' time, alongside 'five fruit and veg a day,' our kids could be chanting comparable mantras for daily emotional wellbeing: do some exercise, do someone a good turn, count your blessings, laugh, savour beauty.*
>
> *We might also be discussing emotional pollution in much the way we now discuss environmental pollution. Top of the list would be advertising … Meanwhile, there would be a strong rationale to increase subsidies for festivals, parks, theatres, community groups, amateur dramatics, choirs and sports clubs.*

This is not hypothetical reasoning in the strict sense. However, it is, in a looser sense, hypothetical, in that it looks at the consequences which might occur *if* we accepted that the state had a role in our happiness. The role of this passage in the argument is to illustrate how a political concern with our emotional well being might develop (in a non-threatening way).

How likely are the hypothetical consequences of allowing the state a role in our emotional wellbeing, and how well does this reasoning support the author's conclusion that, 'the state should resume a role in promoting the good life, not just chivvy us along in the global rat race, anxious and insecure'?

None of the possible consequences examined are unlikely. Chanting mantras, discussing emotional pollutants such as advertising and increasing funding for leisure pursuits such as festivals are all probable. However, they are not necessarily all positive. Children chanting mantras for wellbeing smacks of brainwashing, for example. The author has also omitted consequences that might occur. People are currently demonised for choosing unhealthy lifestyles. The prospect of a similar witch hunt against people who make emotionally unhealthy choices is terrifying. Might our reliance on the government to sort out our emotional lives lead to greater dependency and unhappiness?

So, this scenario provides support for the conclusion to the extent that it sketches realistic possibilities. However, this support is limited.

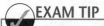
Analogies

Analogy is a pattern of reasoning which claims that two situations are so similar that if we accept a conclusion about one situation, we should also accept it about the other. Analogy is used to make it easier to follow a pattern of thought, to create a clear image to help us understand abstract reasoning or to highlight a pattern shared by two situations or arguments. Quite often we use analogy when we want to show how silly an action or someone's conclusion is.

In *Critical Thinking for OCR Unit 2* we looked at three steps of evaluating an analogy:

1) Identifying the two situations being compared and the conclusion the author wants us to accept on the basis of the analogy.

2) Considering significant similarities and differences between the situations.

3) Deciding whether the situations really are so similar that a conclusion drawn about one can also be drawn about the other.

In Unit 4 you may also have to:

4) Evaluate the support given to the author's reasoning by the analogy. Once you have been through steps 1–3 you will be able to evaluate the support given to a conclusion by an analogy just as you would with any reason.

Evaluating analogies

Let's take an example:

> *Evidence indicates that working long hours is a status symbol indicating a high position in the social pecking order. We may as well say that driving a rusty old car is a status symbol.*

How does the analogy work?

A It suggests that working long hours is considerably less undesirable than having a rusty old car.

B It suggests that our understanding of what gives us status is somewhat confused.

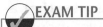

*Multiple choice
questions on
analogies may
include: which
situations are being
compared; what
conclusion the
author is trying to
get you to accept by
using an analogy;
what the similarities
or differences are;
what flaw the
analogy highlights
in the reasoning.*

C It suggests that working long hours does not really confer higher status, just as driving a rusty old car does not confer higher status.

D It suggests that it is silly that status should come through something undesirable like long working hours.

Before trying to decide which of these answers is right, let's work through the four steps of evaluating an analogy.

Identify the two situations being compared and the conclusion the author wants us to accept on the basis of the analogy

The two situations being compared are long working hours leading to high status, and the possibility that driving a rusty car might lead to high status: both are undesirable things. So we are to conclude that it is silly to think that high status should come from something undesirable.

Consider significant similarities and differences between the situations

a) *Similarities*: long working hours used to be a sign of low social status, just like driving a rusty car today. One hundred and fifty years ago, if you worked long hours, it was because you were too poor to support your family any other way. The analogy makes us start thinking about the many ways in which working long hours is bad: it is bad for your health, deprives you of family life and makes unreasonable demands on your time.

b) *Differences*: driving a rusty car is largely undesirable because it shows that you do not have the money for a better car and therefore confers low social status. There isn't anything inherently wrong with driving a rusty car so long as it gets you from A to B safely. On the other hand, long working hours are negative in many ways. This is useful in challenging our understanding of the link between what you do and how much social status you have.

Decide whether the situations really are so similar that a conclusion drawn about one can also be drawn about the other

This analogy has strong emotional impact in making us realise that the link between long working hours and social status is silly, and that our preoccupation with social status might blind us to the down side of working too much. On the other hand, the example of the rusty car which is bad largely because of its implications for your social status makes it rationally less strong.

Evaluate the support given to the author's reasoning by the analogy

We cannot evaluate the impact of this analogy on the overall reasoning until it is embedded in a longer passage.

Now let's look at the four suggested answers in the multiple choice question:

A It suggests that working long hours is considerably less undesirable than having a rusty old car.

The analogy does not do this. You may think this, but we cannot allow our existing opinions to colour our understanding of a passage.

B It suggests that our understanding of what gives us status is somewhat confused.

No – it shows us quite clearly that long working hours have become a status symbol. Our understanding of this is not confused. We may as a society have become confused about what is worth treating as a status symbol, but that is a different issue.

C It suggests that working long hours does not really confer higher status, just as driving a rusty old car does not confer higher status.

No, the analogy suggests that they should not confer high status. It clearly accepts that they do.

D It suggests that it is silly that status should come through something undesirable like long working hours.

Yes.

ACTIVITY 35

a)

> Some philosophers claim that the mind is separate from the body. They describe the relationship between the mind and the body as being like the relationship between a pilot and an aeroplane.

Which of the following expresses a significant difference between these two situations?

A Pilots may fly a range of aeroplanes, whereas my mind may never be in another body.

B I feel as if I make most of the decisions about what my body does just as a pilot decides what an areoplane does.

C My body is clearly physical like an areoplane, whereas my mind appears to be more than physical events.

D My control of my body does not indicate that my mind is separate from the physical body as a pilot is separate from an aeroplane.

b)

> Five annoying housemates, no quick way out, guaranteed fame when you leave. By the time you land on Mars, you'll have been cooped up inside a metal box for 6 months. You won't be able to talk to your friends and family for another two years. You and your fellow inmates are bound to have survived some hair-raising, potentially fatal crises, and everyone's nerves will be in tatters. The pilot won't talk to the engineer. And if that geologist looks at you and rolls his eyes one more time, you'll punch his lights out.
>
> Source: Adapted from New Scientist, 11 March 2006 p.34

What is the force of the reference to reality TV in the first line of the passage?

A It reduces the importance and usefulness of space exploration to that of reality TV.

B It makes it seem as if astronauts only want fame and glory rather than new knowledge.

C It makes the psychological difficulties of space exploration seem real to an earth bound audience.

D It exaggerates the scale of the psychological difficulties experienced by participants in reality TV.

ACTIVITY 36

Evaluate the support given to the main conclusion of the passage below. Support your evaluation by making selective reference to:

- use of and response to counter argument
- use of hypothetical reasoning
- use of analogy.

A group of hard-core grumpies persistently fret about the revival of the St George flag as a symbol of England on the basis that it is associated with violent nationalism and racism. However, the growing acceptance of our national flag is overwhelmingly positive.

A flag is a cultural symbol which has changing meaning according to its use. If we allow the racist connotations of the last century to stop us rallying round our national flag, it will be a victory for the racists. This alone is reason to embrace the flag of St George.

The flag should be a symbol of belonging and unity which draws all the diverse people who call themselves English together. When we see young men of Asian, African and European ancestry shouting together for England, all sporting the red cross on the white background, we see a shawl of unity, draped around the shoulders of the whole nation. We see young saints fighting in common cause against the dragon of racist division.

The grumpies say that flag waving months in advance of a major football tournament is like putting your Christmas tree up months before Christmas. They are simply opposed to joyous celebration of any kind. The flag is the tourist guide's umbrella, pointing the way forward to those who might otherwise be lost and directionless. We should enjoy all that it can offer.

SUMMARY

You should now be able to:

- **evaluate the use of and response to counter argument**
- **evaluate hypothetical reasoning**
- **evaluate the use of analogies.**

Developing your own arguments

Communicating your own ideas in a clear, precise and reasoned way is an important skill, both in Critical Thinking and in life. We all need to be able to support our own opinions or suggested courses of action and deal with opposition to them. Improving your skills in developing your own arguments is the focus of this chapter.

At Critical Thinking AS Level you learned to support a clearly stated conclusion with reasons, evidence and examples in a structured argument. You may have included a short counter argument in your reasoning.

Many of the principles for writing a strong argument at Critical Thinking A2 Level remain the same. You must:

- have a clearly stated conclusion
- consider whether the reasons you give provide strong support for the conclusion you have stated
- structure your argument carefully.

We will revise all these skills, and in particular, we will extend your ability to structure your argument using:

- strands of reasoning
- response to counter argument
- definition of words.

Stating your conclusion clearly

There are two elements to remember when stating your conclusion. These are:

- You must write down your conclusion.
- You must be clear and precise about what your conclusion is.

Writing down your conclusion

In everyday life you will be asked to give or write down your (considered) opinion, answer questions or put forward proposals for action. It is important in these cases that your reasoning does include a statement of your conclusion. People often give reasons, but leave their audience to draw the conclusion for themselves, on the basis that it is obvious. There are three problems with this approach:

1) If you have not stated your conclusion, you will not have provided an argument, but simply some ideas on a theme.

2) What is obvious to you may not be obvious to others.

3) Even if it is obvious that you agree or disagree with a general idea, your precise conclusion may be less clear.

Let's take an example:

> School uniform reduces the bullying that occurs because of individuals' choice of clothing and the amount of money they are able to spend on clothes. It makes getting up in the morning simpler as you do not have to choose what to wear, or look for matching clothes. It acts as a badge of identity, drawing pupils closer together into a community.

In this case, it is clear that the speaker is broadly in favour of school uniform. It is not clear whether the speaker would support any or all of the following claims:

- Schools should consider adopting a school uniform.
- Schools with social problems like bullying should adopt a school uniform.
- School uniform should be compulsory in the sixth form.

These claims are very different, and require different reasoning to support them. So it is important to write your conclusion down. This allows you to check whether you have supported your precise conclusion, and have not just given general support to a vague idea.

Stating your conclusion precisely

In the Critical Thinking A2 exam you will be given a claim to support or challenge. For example, you could be asked to support or challenge the claim that, 'School uniform should be compulsory.'

You have a number of options.

1) You can write an argument which supports or challenges the conclusion as it is, for example:

> School uniform should be compulsory.
>
> School uniform should not be compulsory.

However, these are both very strong conclusions. As we discussed in Chapter 4, a strong conclusion can be weakened by a single example. To make your argument stronger, you may need to make the conclusion weaker. You can remind yourself how to do this by looking at *Critical Thinking for OCR Unit 2*, Chapter 7, p.92.

Either of these strong conclusions may feel too limiting. You may wish to say that neither 4 year-olds nor 18 year-olds should be compelled to wear a uniform, but that 14 year-olds should have to. This leads us onto the second option:

2) You could qualify the conclusion so that you are supporting or challenging it to a certain extent, for example:

> School uniform should be compulsory, but only in secondary schools.
>
> School uniform should not be compulsory except where a school council has voted it in.

A further difficulty might be that there are words in the claim you have been given to support or challenge which are vague or ambiguous. (Refer back to Chapter 5 and *Critical Thinking for OCR Unit 2*, Chapter 6.) So, you now have a third option:

3) You may need or wish to specify or limit the meanings of words and reflect this in your conclusion.

Compulsory might mean any of the following:

- Every schoolchild in the country has to wear a uniform, even those who are home educated.
- Schools must enforce a distinctive uniform on their pupils.
- If a school chooses to have a uniform, pupils must wear it.

Uniform might mean:

- Clothes in the same colour scheme such as a striped blazer and boater with badge, or khakis and beret.
- Girls must wear skirts which end at their knees. Boys must wear trousers which fasten at the waist (not the hips) and end at their ankles. This would be free choice but with restrictions relating to decency and respect for those around us.

So, your conclusion might be:

It should be compulsory for schools to require pupils to wear decent clothing in the same colour scheme at secondary school.

or:

School uniform should be a matter of choice for the school, but where a school imposes a uniform, students should have no leeway at all in modifying it.

or:

Most schools should have uniforms, and require their students to wear them, but it should remain a matter of choice for the school and not be enforced by the government.

We will show how to incorporate discussions of how a word is to be used in your argument later in the chapter.

ACTIVITY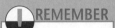

REMEMBER

Consider how strong a claim is. Strong claims need much more support than weak claims.

Consider how you might qualify the following claims if you were asked to support or challenge them. Make sure you are not completely changing the claim.

a) Sixteen year-olds should be given state-funded accommodation.

b) It is wrong to be frivolous.

c) Transport networks should be state run.

d) Happiness should be studied in schools.

e) Investing in further nuclear reactors would be a disaster.

f) People should not wear pink.

g) War is wrong.

h) Children in care should be sent to boarding school.

Supporting your conclusion with reasons

As we discussed at Critical Thinking AS Level and considered in Chapter 1 of this book, reasons must be precisely focused on a conclusion. A reason should give us grounds to accept a conclusion, and should not ramble on about the same topic. Reasons should give strong support to the conclusion. There are two issues here:

- strength of conclusion
- focus of reasons.

Strength of conclusion

Strong conclusions require very strong support. For example:

> *All rap artists promote aggressive behaviour.*

We only need one example of a rap artist who does not promote aggressive behaviour to undermine this claim. It would be very hard to provide support for a claim which did not allow for a counter example. We would have to demonstrate that every single rap artist promoted aggressive behaviour, and even then, we could not allow for new rap artists who were different.

We could make the claim a bit weaker, to make it easier to support:

> *A significant number of rap artists promote aggressive behaviour.*

Several examples and some suggestion that they were typical examples would provide reasonable support for this claim.

What if we weakened the claim further?

> *A few rap artists might promote aggressive behaviour.*

Now we are not saying anything much at all. A few 80 year-old wives of vicars might promote aggressive behaviour. The moon might be made of cheese and inhabited by skiing slot machines. Very little support is required for such weak conclusions – but neither do we learn anything of significance.

Focus of reasons

Evidence must precisely support a reason without leaving gaps in your knowledge, and reasons must be focused on a precise conclusion, not just on the same topic. For example:

> R *John is concerned about the environment.*
>
> C *John should buy an electric car.*

The reason is very general, and does not give a strong reason why John should buy an electric car. If he does not already own a car, or if he flies a great deal, buying an electric car will not help him conserve the environment.

REMEMBER

You could refer back to Chapter 4 of *Critical Thinking for OCR Unit 2*, and Chapters 3 and 4 of this book to remind yourself about how evidence and reasons can support a claim precisely.

At Critical Thinking A2 Level we have extended this idea: looking at an author's work, we may decide that they have provided good support for their intermediate conclusion but have not gone on to provide sufficient support for the move to their main conclusion. For example, in the nuclear power article in Chapter 2 on pages 20–21 we have been looking at, the author provided good support for the intermediate conclusion that, 'The truth is that this form of energy is, in the end, no more safe, reliable or clean than the others.' However, this does not in itself mean that the UK should invest in renewable energy. More work was needed to support the main conclusion.

You can apply the same thinking to your own arguments when you are trying to ensure that you provide good support for your main conclusion. Ask yourself:

> *'Does this reason really mean that I have to accept the main conclusion of my argument?'*

For example:

> *'How well does the fact that school uniforms can help to create a sense of community support the claim that uniforms should be compulsory?'*

ACTIVITY 38

Look again at two claims we considered earlier:

- Schools with social problems, like bullying, should adopt a school uniform.

- School uniform should be compulsory in the sixth form.

a) Brainstorm all your ideas.

b) Write lists of reasons which support and oppose each claim.

c) Consider how the support and opposition for the two claims are different.

d) Write a short argument to support or challenge each of these claims.

ACTIVITY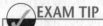

Take one of the claims from Activity 37, which you have qualified.

Write a short argument to support or challenge it.

**EXAM TIP**

In the Critical Thinking A2 exam (Unit 4, Section B), you will be asked to support or challenge a claim which is related to the argument you have been evaluating. There will be a significant number of marks for this task. The longest answers will not necessarily receive the highest marks. You should aim to be clear and concise, and write a short, perceptive, well structured argument in which the reasons support the conclusion. You will not gain more marks by writing more if you have nothing to say.

Argument structure

As you learned at Critical Thinking AS Level, it is important to structure your argument and have some logical progression of ideas, rather than just writing down your ideas as they occur to you. At Critical Thinking AS Level you considered:

!**REMEMBER**

A **strand of reasoning** is a line of thought which has been developed. For example, a reason may be supported with a short argument consisting of reasons, evidence and examples; this would turn it into a strand of reasoning.

- placing your main conclusion at the beginning or end of an argument
- including an intermediate conclusion
- using two to four different reasons
- using evidence or examples to support each reason.

At Critical Thinking A2 Level this still provides the basis of a sound argument structure, but we will look at how to extend it to allow for greater complexity of thought.

Strands of reasoning

One way to extend the Critical Thinking AS Level structure to A2 Level is to use strands of reasoning. In Chapter 1 we looked at identifying strands of reasoning in an author's work.

For example, in her article about happiness in Chapter 2 on pages 23–24, Bunting uses three main strands of reasoning:

1) She establishes happiness as something which can be taken seriously.

2) She shows how the state could be involved in happiness in a (fairly) acceptable way.

3) She shows that the state contributes to our unhappiness.

She draws the conclusion that, 'The state should resume a role in promoting the good life, not just chivvy us along in the global rat race, anxious and insecure.'

The author of the article about nuclear power in Chapter 2 on pages 20–21 had two main strands of reasoning, one of which was broken down into three sub-strands:

1) The claims that nuclear power is clean, reliable and secure are wrong.

   a) clean

   b) reliable

   c) secure

2) Renewable energy seems attractive in comparison with nuclear power.

He concludes that, 'The British Government must not exclude options other than nuclear power.'

Developing your own strands of reasoning

So, how can you create strands of reasoning to structure your argument?

Let's look at the basic model you used for developing your own arguments at Critical Thinking AS Level:

> *'Universities are only able to expand because they are lowering entrance standards.' Counter this claim.*
>
> Source: Adapted from OCR's AS Critical Thinking Paper, January 2006

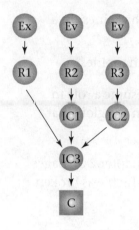

A good AS Level answer might have the following structure:

R1	Wider access from different social groups
Examples	Working people, ethnic minorities
R2	Students more motivated
IC1	Students achieve higher grades
Evidence	Student survey, grades
R3	Teaching improved
IC2	More students achieve highly
Evidence	Grades
IC3	So there are a number of reasons why universities are able to expand which do not depend on granting admission to less able students
C	So universities are not able to expand only because of lower entrance standards.

We can see three strands of reasoning beginning to emerge, relating to wider access, higher motivation among students and better teaching. Each strand of reasoning could be developed further:

1) Show how wider social access allows universities choice of more able students.

2) Support the idea that students are more motivated – why, what evidence?

3) Support the idea that higher motivation leads to higher grades – how?

4) Support the idea that teaching has improved – how?

5) Support the idea that changes in teaching have led to higher grades.

6) Deal with the inevitable counter argument that higher AS and A2 Level grades merely mean a lowering of standards further down the education system (we will look at dealing with counter arguments in more depth later in this chapter).

It is important to remember that each of these points can be developed with a few well chosen words. It is not necessary to write more, but try to make better use of the words you do use.

Worked exercise

Contrast the two following answers:

Answer A

Lots of young people who are studying for A levels today are more motivated than they used to be, which makes them get higher grades than people used to in our parents' generation. So universities can let in a lot of people with high grades and this does not need to be because they are lowering standards. **(57 words)**

Answer B

Young people increasingly understand the social, financial and emotional benefits of studying for a degree, such as meeting friends with similar interests. They are, therefore, increasingly motivated to work hard to master their subjects and so achieve high grades. Students are using their abilities and showing universities they deserve a place. This allows universities a wider choice of able candidates. **(60 words)**

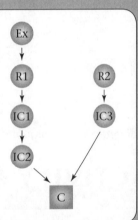

Answer B uses only three more words than Answer A. Yet it is much richer in terms of ideas and structure, as the diagrams show.

Categorising reasons to support ICs

Once we have brainstormed an idea, it is sometimes possible to see that our reasons fall into several different categories. For example:

> *The government should increase funding to improve mental health in the country.*

REMEMBER

You might find it useful to revise the work you did in Chapter 2 of *Critical Thinking for OCR Unit 3*.

Reasons to support this claim might fall into the following categories:

- economic (what it would cost, how much money is available, how much money would be saved, etc.)

- political (whether it would win or lose votes, what else it might lead to)

- moral (is this the right thing to do?).

Each category would form a strand of reasoning with several reasons, examples and evidence to support an intermediate conclusion. The ICs might be:

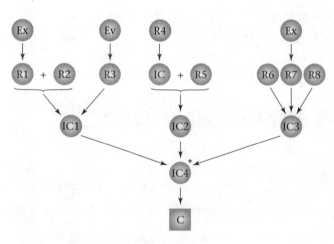

IC1 In economic terms, it would be beneficial to improve mental health.

IC2 Focusing on mental health might be politically damaging.

IC3 Improving mental health would be the right thing to do.

Then you would need to weigh up whether the political negative outweighed the economic and moral positives. This would be another strand of reasoning, leading to a main conclusion.

The diagram of your argument might look like this

ACTIVITY ④⓪

> *'Young people increasingly understand the social, financial and emotional benefits of studying for a degree.'*

a) **Write lists of reasons and evidence to support this claim in the three categories of social, financial and emotional benefits.**

b) **Write a short argument with three clear strands of reasoning to support this claim.**

c) **Work in groups to edit the arguments. Look for unnecessary words, repetition or vagueness. Help each other to improve the clarity of your argument.**

This IC weighs up whether political negative outweighs economic and moral positives

ACTIVITY 41

Write a short argument to support or challenge **one** of the following conclusions. Plan your argument and consider strands of reasoning.

- Public art is a waste of public money.

- Young people should not be exposed to traumatic issues in the classroom.

- Couples should not be allowed to choose the sex of their baby.

- The government should make cars illegal.

Response to counter argument

At Critical Thinking AS Level you probably included a counter reason or short counter argument in your own arguments. You may have done this by stating the opposite of your own conclusion at the beginning of your argument. At A2 Level you will be expected to **respond to counter arguments** and not just to state counter claims.

Write the counter argument down

Make sure that you do write down the counter argument. It will ensure that you are clear about what you are responding to.

A counter argument might support a conclusion which is opposite to or subtly different from your own. On the other hand, it might consist of objections to your own argument. These need to be treated slightly differently.

Reasons to support an opposing argument

Suppose that you want to support the claim:

> *'We have too much choice in modern life.'*

There are strong reasons to support opposite claims which point out/highlight the many benefits of choice. You would need to consider these.

1) Brainstorm lots of ideas to support the conclusion of your argument, and to counter your argument:

Support the argument:

- Having a wide choice of lots of baked beans is just silly.
- Who needs to choose between hundreds of ring tones?
- People can suffer from anxiety about making the wrong choices.
- It is a waste of time choosing silly things such as which rubbish to watch on 146 TV channels.
- Sometimes one option is best: one directory enquiries with one number to remember; just one police force and one fire service.
- It is uncertain whether choice in education is good or bad.

Counter argument:

- Choices make us free and allow us to live our own lives as we wish to.
- Life without choice would be boring and restrictive.
- Choice helps us decide who we really are.
- If we didn't have choices, we would be forced to do lots of things we don't want to do.

2) Select the key points for and against your argument, thinking about strands of argument; for example, some of the points in the list we have written about, such as baked beans, ring tones and TV are very much the same. There is no fixed rule about how many points you should make; in an exam with time pressure, you should probably have about two, three or four strands of reasoning. One of these might be dealing with counter argument.

3) Begin to structure your argument:

R1   Too many choices waste time in a silly way (for example, baked beans, TV, ring tones)

R2   In some cases it may be fatal to have a choice (for example, having one number for the fire services makes it easy to remember in an emergency, whereas the time taken to look up and choose between competing services could mean the difference between life or death)

R3   In other cases, choice can cause problems (for example, health, education)

CA   Choices make us free and allow us to live our own lives as we wish to

R4   (Response to CA) Yes, but not choices about baked beans.

C   So, we have too much choice in modern life.

4) Expand each reason into a strand of reasoning with examples, evidence and further reasons, so that each reason becomes an intermediate conclusion.

5) Write it down.

6) Edit it.

ACTIVITY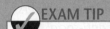

Write a developed version of the argument outlined *to support* the claim that, 'We have too much choice in modern life.'

Now write an argument *to challenge* the claim that, 'We have too much choice in modern life.' Make sure you go through all six steps.

✓ EXAM TIP

When you are writing practice arguments, it is a good idea to give yourself a word limit – say, 150 or 200 words. This should help you to get better at expressing yourself concisely and precisely. In the exam you do not want to waste time counting words; you should be demonstrating that you can write a developed argument without using unnecessary words or repetition.

Objections to your argument

Sometimes, a counter argument might consist of objections to your argument, rather than support for the opposite. These objections might be:

- unacceptable consequences of your argument or proposed course of action
- principles which conflict with your argument or proposed course of action.

Either of these would give us reason not to accept your conclusion, rather than being a positive reason to accept an alternative.

Let's take an example:

> R1   Most crime is committed by young men.
> R2   Most accidents are caused by young men.
> R3   Most anti-social behaviour comes from young men.
> IC   Society suffers from these young men.
> C   Young men should be locked up between the ages of 14 and 24.

Objections to this argument might be:

It is unacceptable to penalise all young men for the offences of a few.

It is unacceptable to lock young men up *before* they have committed an offence.

These are serious objections based on moral principles which have, in theory, been agreed as a basis for our society. They do not offer an alternative solution to the problem of young men's behaviour, or show that young men's behaviour is indeed acceptable. They offer objections to a specific means of dealing with a problem. Let's look at one way of dealing with these objections:

> Society in general suffers greatly from the behaviour of large numbers of young men. Most crime, accidents and incidents of anti-social behaviour are caused by young men. One way of dealing with this would be to keep young men away from society while they are in their destructive phase. Although some liberals will bleat about the unacceptability of penalising all young men for the offences of the few, they miss the point. Locking young men away from society is not a punishment. It is a preventative measure for the benefit of the young men as well as society in general. We are not talking about prison. We are talking about compounds with racing tracks, tuition in fighting, holding your drink and lots of X-boxes with digitally enhanced women who would not be offended by clumsy adolescent chat up lines. All young men are potentially criminal, recklessly dangerous or anti-social. They grow out of it. We have no problems with keeping uranium and plutonium sealed in very safe places. We should have no problems with keeping young men and society completely separate.

This is still a problematic argument. But you are not required to produce an argument which has no problems. You should avoid sweeping generalisations about particular groups of society, such as young men. Despite its flaws, this argument does show how dealing with two objections can make you increase the complexity of your argument.

ACTIVITY 43

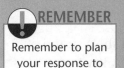
REMEMBER

Remember to plan your response to the objections.

a) **Expand the short argument below into a more complex argument by answering the objections.**

> R1 *Exams cause many young people a great deal of stress.*
> R2 *Many young people do not perform well in exams.*
> IC *Both these groups may suffer for much of their lives because of the exam system.*
> C   *So, young people should not have to take exams.*
>
> *Objections:*
>
> *Exams show what students can do and are a good indicator of what they should do next.*
>
> *The problems suffered by a few students should not be a barrier to the progress and success of the rest.*

b) **Write a short argument to support a claim of your own choice.**

c) **Swap with a partner and think of objections to your partner's argument.**

d) **Consider answers to your partner's objections to your own argument.**

e) **Write a more complex argument including a response to the objections.**

Dealing with words

It is possible – and sometimes necessary – to have a short strand of reasoning which establishes how you are using a few key terms. This will often come near the beginning of an argument.

Let's take an example, 'We would be happier with less choice.'

There are two key terms in this claim which need to be addressed, *happier*, and *choice*. Both could have whole books written about them, but you have to write a short argument which makes it clear how you are using the term.

What do we mean by happier?
We could mean the state of our wellbeing, such as feeling less anxious, feeling fulfilled or even euphoric.

What do we mean by choice?
We could mean economic choice, political choice, personal choice or freedom to choose one course of action over another. Choice could be contrasted to constraint, restraint or limits. There is a significant difference, for example, between choice of profession and choice of brand of baked beans.

> We would be less anxious if we had fewer consumer choices, but happiness includes feeling fulfilled, contented and sometimes joyous. Choice includes being able to make important decisions about your own life, not just whether to download the Star Wars theme tune or James Blunt's latest line.

ACTIVITY

Write a short argument to support or challenge one of the following claims:

• Religion is a tool of oppression.

• Heroism is not restricted to the battlefield.

• Britain should return plundered artworks to their countries of origin.

! REMEMBER

Remember, when you are writing your own arguments, to check that you have considered:

• strands of reasoning

• counter argument

• definition of terms

• that everything is clearly stated.

Remember too that you can use principles in your arguments, as you have done in Unit 3. A principle can act as a reason, intermediate conclusion or conclusion in an argument.

SUMMARY

You should now be able to write concise, precise and relevant arguments which:

• **are structured using strands of reasoning**

• **anticipate and respond to counter argument**

• **define any vague terms**

• **state reasons, conclusions and counter argument clearly and precisely.**

In Chapters 1–7 you have developed and extended the skills of analysis of argument, evaluation of reasoning and development of your own reasoning. In this chapter you will consider strategies that you can use to help you apply these skills to answering exam questions.

Before the exam

In Critical Thinking there is very little content to learn. What you have done mostly during the course is to acquire skills. You can apply these skills to any subject matter. There are a few things you can learn, however. These include:

- key terms
- names, explanations and examples of flaws.

As part of your preparation you should also:

- read the newspapers. This will make you familiar with the level of language and debate required at Critical Thinking A2. It will improve your general knowledge and make you familiar with the kind of topic which might come up in the exam.
- train yourself to read quickly and precisely. A good way to do this is to read as much as you can.

Finally, there are very specific kinds of exam practice you will find useful, including:

- Make sure you are familiar with the kinds of question you might come across and the answers required. Use past papers and mark schemes.
- Every time your work is marked, compare your answers to answers in the mark scheme or which gained high marks. Don't be downhearted by your mark – look for ways to improve it.
- Work with a friend. Mark each other's answers and then take it in turns to explain why you have given the marks you have. Listen carefully to the explanations given.

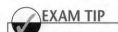

EXAM TIP

Reading quickly and precisely is a key exam skill. In Critical Thinking every word counts, and candidates who misread a question often end up with 0 marks.

- Practise.
- Practise again.
- Practise some more.

The exam

The Unit 4 exam paper lasts for 1 hour and 45 minutes. It is divided into:

Section A   20 multiple choice questions (allow 40 minutes)

Section B   One longer passage with:

Analysis questions

Evaluation questions

Developing your own reasoning to support or challenge a claim related to the main passage

General exam strategies

Think of the exam as a game which has to be played by certain rules. Think how you can make those rules work to your advantage. By doing this you can maximise your chances of doing as well as you possibly can.

- **Read the questions carefully!**

    The most important thing you can do is read carefully in the exam. No matter how profound your thinking, or how wonderful your reasoning, you will gain 0 marks if you have answered a question that hasn't been asked. Candidates lose too many marks by not reading carefully.

- **Answer the questions in the order that suits you**

    You do not have to start at question 1 and complete each question in order. When you are practising, work out which bits of the paper you find it easiest to gain marks in. Do those sections first. So long as you label each answer clearly, it does not matter which order you do them in. For example, many candidates find that they gain their best marks in class in the questions on developing their own arguments. These questions are usually at the end of a paper, so candidates sometimes do not reach them. If you are one of these people, why not try writing your own arguments as soon as you have read the passage, or after you have finished the analysis questions?

REMEMBER

Analyse means break an argument down into reasons, intermediate conclusions, unstated assumptions and so on, and indicate the structure.

Evaluate means say how good the reasoning is, considering flaws in the reasoning, rhetorical persuasion, use of evidence and examples and so on.

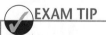

EXAM TIP

When developing your own argument you need to be careful that you don't repeat or attack the argument from the passage.

- **Time yourself carefully**

  Make sure that you leave yourself enough time to attempt every question on the paper. You cannot get marks for a question you have not answered at all.

  There comes a point for each question when you have gained as many marks as you can, and need to move on to the next question. You may spend an extra 5 minutes on 1 question, but only gain 1 extra mark. If you move on to the next question, you may gain 7 marks in those 5 minutes.

  Knowing how long you are likely to need for each question is particularly important if you answer questions in the order that suits you.

- **Think quality not quantity**

  Most questions in Unit 4 Section B are marked using descriptions of levels of performance. So, for example, you may be rewarded for having a 'clear' understanding of strength and weakness in an argument. Writing more will not necessarily move you up a level. To reach a higher level you would need to demonstrate a 'sound, thorough and perceptive evaluation' of strength and weakness in an argument.

Strategies for multiple choice questions in Section A

- **Read the passages carefully**

  At Critical Thinking A2 Level there will be a greater range of multiple choice questions. Unlike at AS Level, where there are six basic question types, at A2 Level you will not have seen all the question types before. One of the skills being tested is your ability to think in unpredicted ways. So it is important to read the questions carefully to be sure you really know what the question is asking you to do.

- **Read the passage before the answers**

  Read the passage before you look at the suggested answers. You should have an idea what the answer might be before you look at the answers. If you have read the answers, you might be trying to make one of them fit the passage rather than deciding which is the correct answer.

- **Identify the main conclusion**

  It is always worth making sure you know what the main conclusion of an argument is, whatever the question is asking you to do. For example, if you are identifying a flaw, this is a problem somewhere between the reasons and the conclusion, so it helps to know what the conclusion is.

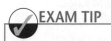

EXAM TIP

Use a light pencil line to cross wrong answers out, just in case you do decide you need to read them again!

- **Eliminate answers**

  It is often possible to eliminate one or two multiple choice answers quite easily. Cross the answers out on the question paper, so only the answers you think might be right can easily be seen. This will stop you unnecessarily reading answers again after you have decided they are wrong. Then you can concentrate on just two answers.

- **Justify your decision**

  Explain to yourself why the wrong answers are wrong. Give reasons why the right answers are right. With practice, you should be able to do this quickly.

- **Guess and move on**

  If you are spending more than a minute and a half on a question, guess and move on. Leave an asterisk (*) by the answer to remind yourself to check it later. You have a 25% chance of getting the answer right if you guess. You will certainly get it wrong if you leave a blank. You will almost certainly lose marks if you spend too long on one question, because you won't get to the questions you can do.

- **Check that each answer is in the right space**

  Do make sure you write the answers down in the right space on the form. If you leave a blank, then fill it in with the answer to the next question, ALL your answers after this will be in the wrong spaces.

- **Consider splitting the multiple choice questions into two blocks**

  Some people find 20 multiple choice questions at once a bit mind boggling, and after the first few, all the answers look equally good. If your time management is good, why not do 10, then look at section B, and make sure you have time later to go back to the rest of the multiple choice?

Section A

SAMPLE QUESTION

Almost all of us have fantasised about rising above congestion on a jetpack and floating through empty skies to our destination. There are, however, too many problems in real life. The rocket belt used at the opening of the 1984 Olympics had a maximum flight time of 25 seconds, even with full tanks. A man from Sussex has experienced many hazards whilst making and flying his own rocket pack. He nearly died in an accident during testing. A large section of the M25 was closed when the lorry delivering the hydrogen peroxide for this rocket pack burst into flames. This combination of danger and limited flight time means that jetpacks are only ever going to be the plaything of the few.

Source: OCR Critical Thinking Unit 4 Critical Reasoning Paper, June 2006

a) Which of the following best expresses the main conclusion of the above argument?

   A   Jetpacks are simply too unsafe and impractical.

   B   Jetpacks will remain purely in the realm of fantasy.

   C   Jetpacks are just big boys' toys.

   D   Jetpacks will only be used by a small number of people.

b) 'That's like people in the 1950s who thought that only a few people would ever own a personal computer.'

   How does this analogy highlight a flaw in the above argument?

   A   It shows how technology can change over time to make things cheaper and available to more people.

   B   It demonstrates that technology can change over time to overcome difficulties which prevent mass consumption of an item.

   C   It assumes that changes in technology over time will make the jetpack available to everyone.

   D   It generalises from computers to jetpacks, just as the above argument generalises from a few examples about jetpacks.

Analysis of argument in sample question

Context   Almost all of us have fantasised about rising above congestion on a jetpack and floating through empty skies to our destination.

E.g. 1   The rocket belt used at the opening of the 1984 Olympics had a maximum flight time of 25 seconds, even with full tanks.

E.g. 2   A man from Sussex has experienced many hazards while making and flying his own rocket pack. He nearly died in an accident during testing. A large section of the M25 was closed when the lorry delivering the hydrogen peroxide for this rocket pack burst into flames.

R1   There are, however, too many problems in real life – combination of danger and limited flight time

C   Jetpacks are only ever going to be the plaything of the few.

Justification of answers to sample question

a) Which of the following best expresses the main conclusion of the above argument?

For this part of the question, it is clearly necessary to know what the conclusion of the argument is.

Answer: D Jetpacks will only be used by a small number of people.

This rephrases the conclusion.

A Jetpacks are simply too unsafe and impractical.

This is a reason to support the conclusion.

B Jetpacks will remain purely in the realm of fantasy.

This exaggerates. For most of us they may, but there are already examples of jetpack-like things being used.

C Jetpacks are just big boys' toys.

This is based on a misinterpretation of plaything of the few. It misses the important aspect that not many people will ever use them.

b) 'That's like people in the 1950s who thought that only a few people would ever own a personal computer.'

How does this analogy highlight a flaw in the above argument?

This question is very much more difficult than part a). You need to make sure you are answering the question, not just identifying a flaw.

Answer: B It demonstrates that technology can change over time to overcome difficulties which prevent mass consumption of an item.

The stimulus passage is flawed in that it moves from past technological difficulties to the exclusion of future developments – these difficulties mean that the jetpack will only ever be the plaything of the few. By highlighting a similar perception about computers which we know to have been proved false, we can see the flaw in this reasoning. This does not mean that jetpacks will become readily available.

A It shows how technology can change over time to make things cheaper and available to more people.

The issue with jetpacks is not cost – but danger and technological inefficiency. So, although one reason why computers have become more available is the lower cost, it is changes in technology which have made the difference.

C It assumes that changes in technology over time will make the jetpack available to everyone.

Not to everyone. Not an assumption – an analogy. If it assumes anything it is that the two situations are parallel. Furthermore, this is too definite.

D It generalises from computers to jetpacks, just as the above argument generalises from a few examples about jetpacks.

No it doesn't. The comment about computers makes a point about changing technology and our opinions, which can be applied to jetpacks. This is not generalising.

Section B

You should have 1 hour and 5 minutes for this part of the paper. There are 65 marks allocated for the questions. This is roughly a mark a minute, but you do have to spend time reading the passage.

- First, read the passage carefully.
- Make sure you can identify the main conclusion.
- Read the questions carefully.
- Check how many questions there are, and how many marks you get for each. It will not necessarily be the same every year.

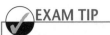

EXAM TIP

There are also 5 marks for the quality of your written communication. These will be given for clear, succinct and precise communication of good Critical Thinking points.

- Divide your time carefully. If a question is worth 9 marks, it does not make sense to spend 20 minutes on it.
- Do not be too perfectionist. The examiners know that you have a lot to do, and are looking for good answers under exam conditions. It is impossible to write thoroughly about everything. It is possible to get top marks even if you haven't written everything that could be written. You need to select key points to make, make them well, and move on.

Questions worth nine marks or more are marked using levels of description. Details of these levels can be found in the mark schemes, but all of them share a common framework:

Level 4   Sound, perceptive and thorough analysis/evaluation/ reasoning

Level 3   Clear understanding/clear, effective reasoning

Level 2   Basic understanding/reasoning

Level 1   Limited understanding/reasoning

Level 0   Nothing worth crediting.

As a rough guide, it seems reasonable to assume that a candidate should have a 'basic' understanding in order to meet the requirements to gain a pass in an A level.

All the sample questions that follow refer to the happiness text, found on pages 23–24.

Analysis questions

There are two main question types you are likely to find in the analysis part of Section B.

1) **Name and briefly explain the function of the following element in the structure of the author's argument (see page 23): Happiness will be taken more seriously.**

    Student A: This is an intermediate conclusion, which gives support to the idea that the state can play a role in the good life.

    Examiner's comment: This is a good answer. 2 marks.

    Student B: Evidence

    Examiner's comment: This answer gets 0 marks. It is not evidence.

2) Analyse in detail the structure of the reasoning in paragraph 7 by identifying reasons, intermediate conclusions, etc.

Student A: The first reason stated by the author is the comparison between emotional and environmental pollution. She then makes an unfounded claim that advertising would be top of the list. She wrongly states that advertising is bad for us rather than promoting our free choice before coming to a conclusion which rounds off the paragraph, reinforcing her main point with examples.

Examiner's comment: This candidate has a very limited understanding of how the structure of the argument works in this paragraph and has failed to understand the relationships of support between reasons and conclusions. They have not even identified which part of the argument is the conclusion of this paragraph. They have also mixed analysis and evaluation. They have, however, correctly identified that examples are used at the end of the paragraph.

Student B: The main conclusion of this paragraph is that we might be discussing emotional pollution like we discuss environmental pollution. This is supported by a reason, that advertising is bad for our emotional health because it induces dissatisfaction and the author has given some examples.

Examiner's comment: This candidate is on the borderline between basic and clear understanding of the passage. They have identified the main conclusion of the passage, and correctly said that it is supported by the idea that advertising is bad for our emotional health. However they have included the reason which supports the intermediate conclusion as part of the same element rather than showing that one supports the other. The candidate has identified examples but has not said what the author is doing with these examples.

For an analysis of this paragraph, see the guidance to Activity 10b.

When you are analysing an argument, the skill being tested is whether you know which bit of the author's work is a reason, which is an intermediate conclusion, etc. It takes longer to paraphrase than to reproduce the author's words.

Evaluation question

You are likely to find questions which ask you to evaluate the support given to a particular claim, or which ask about a specific aspect of the author's argument. *You will access the highest marks by making sure you answer the questions precisely. It may be tempting to just list flaws, but you must ensure that you relate all your answers to the specific question posed.*

1) Evaluate the support given by the reasoning in paragraphs 2–4 to the claim that, 'Happiness will be taken seriously.'

Student A: There is only limited support given to the claim that 'happiness will be taken seriously.' In paragraph 3 the author refers to unspecified research, and claims that happiness has been tagged to intellectual disciplines. If we accept the assumption that intellectual disciplines are taken seriously, we can also accept that happiness can be taken seriously. This is a weaker claim than that it will be taken seriously.

Paragraph 2 shows that we have become much unhappier by a range of measures, and paragraph 4 shows that unhappiness (which is conflated with mental ill health) is expensive. Both of these give us a reason why unhappiness should be taken seriously, which is different from the claim that happiness will be taken seriously.

Examiner's comment: This is a sound, thorough and perceptive evaluation of the strength and weakness of the reasoning in paragraphs 2–4.

Student B: The author conflates unhappiness and mental ill health, treating them as if they were the same. However, you can be unhappy without having a mental illness, and people with mental illnesses can be happy. The author assumes in paragraph 2 that criminals are unhappy people, which is not necessarily the case. Carrying out a successful robbery might give some people a buzz, just like scoring a goal for England. The author states that mental ill health costs the country £9 billion. This effectively supports the claim that 'happiness will be taken seriously.

Examiner's comment: This candidate shows a basic understanding of weakness in the reasoning. They have accurately identified the conflation of unhappiness and mental ill health, but have not evaluated its impact on the reasoning. The point is taken in isolation. The candidate's second point is not accurate. The author does not assume that criminals are unhappy people; she states that crime is a measure of unhappiness, so all she needs to assume is that crime can be a symptom of unhappiness. The candidate's third point is going in the right direction but it is not clear how this evidence supports the claim. Just repeating a point and stating 'this effectively supports a claim' does not demonstrate clear understanding.

Developing your own reasoning questions

Questions on developing your own reasoning are likely to ask you to support or challenge a claim which is either:

- in the argument but not strongly supported
- closely related to the argument, but not actually in the argument.

You MUST write your own argument, using your own reasoning. Repetitions of the argument from the passage cannot be credited.

Remember quality is more important than quantity. Think about your answers before you write them down.

1) If individuals cannot make good choices, the state must make choices for individuals. Write your own argument to support or challenge this claim.

Student A: The concept of choice becomes pointless if someone has already decided what you should choose, and is going to take over if you make the wrong choice. This is no choice at all. In a democracy it is important that we should be able to make real and important choices about our own lives.

Sometimes society suffers from people's choices. For example, if someone repeatedly commits murder, they have to go to prison where they can't choose to murder. Or if people binge drink and throw up in the street and make lots of noise which affects other people perhaps they should be encouraged to make better choices.

Sometimes people suffer from their own choices. If someone marries an attractive person, then discovers they are not very nice, it was their own choice, but they might suffer. If a person lives on junk food and has a heart attack they are suffering from their own choices.

Examiner's comment: This candidate has made some perceptive comments, particularly in the first paragraph. This candidate has two distinct categories of choices which cause problems – for society and for ourselves, and has provided useful examples. However, there is no stated conclusion and it is not even clear whether the candidate intended to support or challenge the claim. This is not an argument, so, despite its good points, it can only be rewarded as limited.

Student B: In general, the state must not make choices for individuals, even if individuals make bad choices. It may be argued that the state should make choices for us if our choices have serious consequences for others, for society in general, or for ourselves. Murderers, for example should not be allowed to continue to choose to murder. People who persistently make bad choices about their health might have to pay for their health care.

However, these are not really cases of the state making choices for us. Murderers have their right to choose removed for the safety of others, and people who make bad choices may have to face the consequences of their choices. But this is not the same as the state actually making choices for us, such as making us eat vegetables every day.

Whilst the state can attempt to influence our decisions through laws and advertising campaigns, it cannot and should not attempt to make decisions for us. We live in a democracy and we have the rights to liberty, privacy and freedom of speech. Our ancestors have fought oppressive rulers over hundreds of years to gain these rights and we should look after them. If we look at other countries we can see how invasive governments can be when they try to take choice away from individuals.

Examiner's comment: This candidate has come to a clear conclusion. They have anticipated and responded perceptively to counter argument and given some reasons which provide some support for their conclusion. They have perhaps spent too long on the counter argument rather than on developing their own reasoning, and their own reasoning is less well structured and less perceptive. This response is on the borderline between clear and sound, perceptive and thorough.

Please note that there are no suggested answers for Activities 1, 9, 16, 25, 28 and 37–44 because they do not have one recommended answer; answers may vary.

ACTIVITY ❷

a)   Answer: B

(R1) Maggots eat dead flesh. (R2) Maggots can reduce the risk of amputation significantly. (R3) Maggots can be produced in a sterile way. (C) Maggots are a good method of cleaning infected wounds.

A   Three unconnected statements of opinion.

C   Explanation.

D   Rant. This is an opinion about fitness centres, followed by an alternative version of what fitness centres do. No support is offered.

b)   Answer: D

(CA) This research has not come up with a convincing, reproducible explanation of the paranormal. (R) It has produced some interesting findings about the way the brain works. (C) Scientific research into the paranormal is useful and valuable.

A   Recommendation and two statements. No reasons to persuade us to agree with the recommendation.

B   Explanation.

C   Definition/description.

ACTIVITY ❸

Evidence: Research suggests that there is a sleep trigger, which slows down in adolescence.

R1   This makes it difficult for teenagers to go to sleep early.

R2   This is also why teenagers struggle to get up early.

A   Struggling to get up early means at any point during the morning.

A   It is unfair to ask teenagers to struggle.

IC   This means that it is unfair to expect teenagers to attend morning lessons.

A   Teenagers' struggles with mornings outweigh other considerations (e.g. staff's different biological requirements).

C   So schools and colleges should rearrange their working days to start after lunch and finish during the evening.

ACTIVITY ➍

Context: Freedom of speech is a fundamental part of democracy. Principle: It is important that we may say what we think, even if others disagree with us.

But:

R1   (Analogy) Being entitled to carry a gun does not entitle you to kill and maim other people at random.

IC   So we should not abuse this freedom (of speech).

C   So, preventing people from persistently ridiculing a group of people, or prohibiting incitement to religious or racial hatred, does not go against the principle of free speech. It merely puts civilised limits on its use.

ACTIVITY ➎

a) C

b) D

ACTIVITY ➏

a) B

b) C

c) CA Although allowing nurses to prescribe medicines ought to allow people easier access to routine medication.

R1 It takes a doctor more than seven years to thoroughly understand how the human body works, and what effects various doses of drugs can have on it.

R2 Nurses do not learn in the same detail.

IC They simply do not know enough to take charge of prescribing drugs.

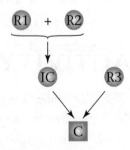

Note: It is not normal to represent a counter argument in a diagram.

R3   Furthermore, prescription is an unfair burden of responsibility to lay on people who have chosen a caring rather than a diagnostic role.

C   It is a disaster waiting to happen.

The main strand of reasoning relates to nurses' knowledge. The idea of responsibility has not been developed into a strand of reasoning.

ACTIVITY 7

Ex   Controversy was recently generated over a rock sculpture called *Monolith and Shadow* commissioned to stand outside a new London hospital.

Ex   It was described as a '£70,000 pebble' by the down-market press.

(Assumed counter argument)   Public art is a waste of money.

R1   But this only served to demonstrate their knowledge of the price of everything and the value of nothing.

R2   Public art, whether commissioned by the public or private sector, has the capacity to enhance our cities and our quality of life.

C   *Alison Lapper Pregnant* is a welcome addition to our capital's collection of artistic riches.

R1   dismisses an assumed counter argument supported by the example of the reaction to *Monolith and Shadow*. R2 states what the author believes to be the case. A generous interpretation of the text would suggest that R2 is supported by some of the reasoning in the earlier paragraphs; our quality of life might be improved by looking at beautiful and thought- provoking works of art. R2 gives support to the conclusion.

ACTIVITY 8

Ev   They (independent energy experts) say that at the present rate of use, worldwide supplies of rich uranium ore will soon become exhausted, perhaps within the next decade.

R1   Nuclear power stations of the future will have to rely on second-grade ore, which requires huge amounts of conventional energy to mine it.

Ev   For each tonne of poor-quality uranium, some 5000 tonnes of granite will have to be mined, milled and then disposed of.

R2 (hypothetical) This could rise to 10,000 tonnes if the quality deteriorates further.

IC1 At some point, and it could happen soon, the nuclear industry will be emitting as much carbon dioxide from mining and treating its ore as it saves from the 'clean' power it produces thanks to nuclear fission.

IC2 (Assumed) So, nuclear power is not as clean as is claimed.

IC3 These (three) claims are at best specious, at worst untrue.

ACTIVITY

(3 claims)

a)

i) Is an intermediate conclusion from the first strand of reasoning. The idea that happiness will be taken seriously makes it possible for the state to intervene.

ii) This is a counter argument, responding to the idea that the state might have a role in our emotional life.

iii) This is a reason to support the intermediate conclusion that the state is part of the problem.

iv) This is the main conclusion.

b)

R1 Advertising induces dissatisfaction with its invidious comparisons with an affluent elite.

IC1 Advertising is bad for our emotional health.

IC2 (Assumed) So things which are emotionally bad for us can be seen as emotional pollutants.

IC3 So we might also be discussing emotional pollution in much the way we now discuss environmental pollution.

The last sentence provides an alternative to polluting activities, and an example of a way in which the state might usefully intervene in our emotional lives.

ACTIVITY 11

a) We can conclude with some certainty that Funmilola has scalded her arm and should put it under cold water. We can conclude that she may need medical attention.

b)   We can conclude with some certainty that Kamal is likely to crash, either accidentally or in controlled conditions to stop the car. We can be fairly sure that he will be injured.

ACTIVITY ⑫

a)   Answer: B. **If drugs can erase the memories, guilt and trauma associated with bad actions, we may be more likely to repeat the bad actions. So, there are questions about how ethically acceptable these drugs are.**

   A   The availability of the drugs does not mean that everyone will have access to them.

   C   They are, but this is not a conclusion which can be drawn from the evidence. It is a reason to oppose the introduction of such drugs.

   D   This statement is too strong.

b)   Answer: C. **The graph is drawn in £ per week disposable income at 2002/3 prices. So an average household had more disposable income in 2003 than 1971. Disposable income has a strong link to standards of living. The median household is a bit more than £100 a week better off (about half as much again), whilst the best off are more than £300 a week better off (about double).**

   A   No, it has risen more for the richest.

   B   We have information about household disposable income, which is not the same as the nation's wealth.

   D   No, standards of living have increased for everyone.

ACTIVITY ⑬

a)   We need to know how much water Funmilola has spilled – a splash or a lot. We need to know how to treat burns.

b)   We need to know how well and knowledgeably Kamal drives, and how calm his nerves are in a crisis.

ACTIVITY ⑭

Answer: B. **If several tonnes of waste were needed to power a small fan for a short time, it seems unlikely that this source of energy could keep our cars on the roads.**

   A   If this process turned out to be efficient, chocolate waste could be converted to energy in chocolate factories.

   C   This is irrelevant. The chocolate is being made anyway.

   D   The current availabilty of hydrogen-powered fuel cells is irrelevant; perhaps more can be made.

ACTIVITY ⓯

'Abortion should be discouraged.'

Strengthen: d, e, f, i   Weaken: a, c, g, h   Neither strengthen nor weaken: b

ACTIVITY ⓱

Answer: D. **This gives us a possible medical use of mesoscopic devices, which does not give us a reason why engineers in general should or should not understand mesoscopic devices.**

A   strengthens the claim by showing why it is important for engineers to understand the mesoscopic world.

B   strengthens the claim by highlighting a significant difference between forces at human and mesoscopic scale.

C   weakens the argument, giving a reason why only some engineers need to know about mesoscopic forces.

ACTIVITY ⓲

Answer: B would not explain how the groups in the conventional classroom lost less weight. A, C and D would explain.

ACTIVITY ⓳

One possible answer might include the following points:

The author's argument is based more on ideas and speculative possibilities than on evidence, and where evidence is used, it is waved at with a flourish rather than solidly incorporated into the argument.*

The claim that happiness has gone respectable so it will be taken more seriously depends on a reference to unspecified research. The author quotes the science of happiness and happiness economics as intellectual disciplines to support her claim that happiness will be taken more seriously. These 'intellectual' disciplines may not lead the sceptic to take happiness seriously, any more than 'the science of magic', or 'boogiebum economics.'

---

*   In a journalistic piece about a very abstract concept, happiness, this use of evidence is not necessarily a devastating flaw, but from a Critical Thinker's point of view it is a weakness.

The author's claim that unhappiness is an expensive business is supported by evidence relating to mental ill health, and depends on the assumption that mental ill health and unhappiness are the same thing/similar. The costs of mental ill health are certainly great, and these give us a reason to take mental health, and the lack of it, seriously. However, we need to be convinced that this evidence actually relates to the author's argument about happiness.

Ideas from a single work about the science of happiness are used extensively towards the end of the argument. The credibility of the source – Layard – is uncertain. The loss of two predictors of happiness, given without any attempt to describe or define happiness, does not in itself support the further claim that this 'leaves the market a free rein to describe happiness – the new car, new sofa, new holiday – and to manipulate our insecurities around status.' The claim is probably as good a description of our society as many others, but the evidence from Layard barely supports it.

Overall, then, the author's work gains superficial credibility by referring to research and using statistics. However, the only claim that is truly supported by evidence is that 'mental ill health is expensive,' and that does not relate directly to her argument. This is a shame because her ideas are extremely interesting.

ACTIVITY 20

a)   A is valid. B is invalid. Some people who are entitled to use the LRC are not students (e.g. staff).

b)   The valid argument is B.

ACTIVITY 21

The correct answer is A.

1)   **All students who went on the French exchange gained B or better. Blanche gained a C. So Blanche did not go on the French exchange.**

3)   **All students who went on the French exchange gained B or better. Alice went on the French exchange. So Alice must have gained an A or B.**

However, we do not know that everybody who got an A or B went on the French exchange. So Siobhán may not have been on the exchange, and Leigh may have gained an A or B even though she did not participate.

ACTIVITY ㉒

To move from the evidence that over 600,000 staff have been added to the public sector to the reason that the state is inefficient, bloated and burdened by pointless bureaucracy, it is necessary to assume that:

- the state was not under-staffed in 1997

- the state is inefficient *because* there are too many people working in it

- the additional workers are not workers such as teachers and nurses.

All of these assumptions could be challenged. If they were, then the reason could be challenged.

To move from the state being inefficient and burdened to the conclusion that the state sector should be reduced, it is necessary to assume that:

- reducing the state sector will make it more efficient

- a reduction of the state sector would mean losing bureaucratic overlap rather than teachers and nurses.

Again, we could challenge both these assumptions. The state would have to be reduced in the right way to make it more efficient. It would be easier to reduce it by reducing the numbers of teachers and nurses than to reorganise it such that it was efficient. It is also necessary to ignore (or accept) the outcome of unemployment; if one in four people works in the public sector, a significant reduction in the public sector workforce would lead to a significant rise in unemployment.

You have to assume that it is a bad thing for one in four working adults to be employed by the state sector; but this is not in itself evidence that the state is inefficient.

The claim that the state is inefficient and burdened by pointless bureaucracy, if it were supported, is a key reason to support the conclusion. It would give us a reason to make the state more efficient. But as we have seen, reducing its size may not make the state more efficient.

The examples of incompetence in government departments do not show that Britain is no better governed. Evidence of problems now does not mean that problems in 1997 were not worse. The evidence is also selective: it is mostly chosen from government departments rather than the wider state sector. A number of private projects have run into funding trouble as bad as the NHS computer. Again, if Britain is no better governed, this does not mean that the public sector as such should be reduced. It might simply mean that the policy makers (the politicians we voted in) should be replaced.

Overall, then, the reasons give only weak support to the conclusion, and depend on a number of assumptions which can be challenged.

ACTIVITY ㉓

a)   The argument assumes that:

   - the Divorce Reform Act has caused the rise in the divorce rate

   - divorce is the cause of family breakdown.

   However, there are many other factors which contribute to a rising divorce rate, including changing attitudes to marriage, and women having enough money to survive without a man's income. As the Act made it easier to divorce, it probably did contribute to the increase in divorces, even if it wasn't the main cause of divorce. Equally, divorce contributes to but is not the only cause of family breakdown. Some families break down through crime or bereavement for example. So, the conclusion that this law has led directly to family breakdown is weakly supported, as the reasoning depends on two assumptions of causal effect which can only be partly accepted. But a weaker conclusion that the Divorce Reform Act contributed to family breakdown can certainly be accepted.

b)   The argument generalises from behaviour in two studies which shows that monkeys may help each other out to an idea of fairness as instinctive and common to primates. The conclusion is far more general than the evidence allows.

c)   The author's suggestion that, 'the fact that events coincide does not mean that there is a causal link between them', does not demonstrate that there is NOT a causal connection between industrialisation and global warming. They also discount other evidence, such as the nature of carbon dioxide, which would explain how industrialisation might cause global warming, and show the parallel with voting to be weak. The author also attacks the arguer rather than the argument. This leaves the conclusion very poorly supported.

d)   This argument is not flawed. The estate agent has been inconsistent; it cannot be true that they sent all the details to the website on Friday, if all the details included a photo of the house with a for sale sign that didn't go up until the following Wednesday. So the estate agent's inconsistency is a reason to support the conclusion that the estate agent wasn't telling the truth (or at least not the whole truth).

ACTIVITY 24

Some, but not all, of the points you may have made include:

a) The argument assumes that the only duties we have are those we have voluntarily undertaken. However, we have many duties, such as obeying the law and respecting the rights of others which we do not have a choice about. So a desire to avoid a duty does not support the conclusion that there is no duty.

The argument assumes that we are not responsible for the consequences of our actions if we have done our best to avoid them. This is problematic because there are some circumstances in which we are held to be responsible for the consequences of our actions even though they are unintentional, such as manslaughter or driving without due care and attention. We use contraceptives and have sex in the knowledge that a pregnancy is still possible. So, although we are taking measures to prevent this consequence, the excuse that, 'I didn't mean to' can only reduce, not remove responsibility. This further weakens the support for the conclusion that a woman has no duty to the foetus.

The author of the argument restricts the options to taking the risk of pregnancy or 'living like a nun'. The author is responding to an anticipated counter argument, that women who do have sex have not done 'all' they can to avoid becoming pregnant. A middle option allowing for intimacy without risk (use your own imaginations!) however, weakens this response. This weakness would not be fatal to the argument but in addition to the other weaknesses, it means that there is very little support for the main conclusion.

b) There is very weak support for the conclusion that, 'we should take no notice of those extreme liberals who want to ensure that terrorists receive a fair trial.' The argument assumes that all those tried for terrorist acts are in fact guilty. Those who have not committed terrorist acts, but are accused of them, certainly deserve a fair trial. The conflict between the rights of those who are injured in terrorist attacks and the rights of those accused of terrorist acts does not mean that the accused should forfeit their rights. It does mean that we should think carefully about the balance. Suggesting that terrorists do not care about the rights of their victims, so we should not care about their right to a fair trial, is an example of reasoning from wrong actions. Their lack of concern for us is not a good reason for us not to care about them. So this conclusion is not supported by this reasoning.

ACTIVITY 26

a)   The appeal to Adam Smith is a good one. He is not used to end argument; his words are used to support an argument. Smith was an economist – often referred to as the founding father of economics. Although he was writing 200 years ago, his point is still relevant. The workers need their wages more urgently than a company needs a particular worker. The appeal to Smith's authority is particularly strong because it would normally be big companies who would refer to Adam Smith, rather than trade unions.

b)   The appeal to tradition in this passage is quite reasonable. There is no suggestion that tradition is the only reason to keep the office of Lord Chancellor. The reasoning is that there should be consultation and debate before such a long standing tradition is dispensed with; we are also told that this tradition has worked (ensuring the stability and fairness of our judicial system). So, because tradition is taken into consideration but not used as the only reason not to change, this appeal to tradition is a reasonable part of the argument and not a flaw.

ACTIVITY 27

In the article on nuclear power, the author appeals to the authority of 'two independent experts, one a chemist and energy specialist, the other a nuclear physicist." We are unsure who these two people are, so we cannot easily check if they are reliable experts working in respected institutions. We are told that they are independent, so they ought not to have strong vested interests. Indeed, the nuclear physicist might be thought to have a vested interest to promote the use of nuclear technology, so the fact that they are arguing that nuclear energy is not safe, reliable or secure increases their credibility. It is possible that these two people may disagree with expert opinion in general. However, even if this were the case, it would not necessarily make them wrong. At all times, evidence from these sources is quoted, so the appeal to authority is not there just to end argument. In theory, although the subject matter is complex, it would be possible to check their evidence.

Furthermore, the additional appeal to the authority and evidence of 'the energy writer Fleming' and 'MIT (Massachusetts Institute of Technology)' corroborate the evidence from the two independent experts. MIT in particular is a well regarded institution which should check that research is properly conducted. So the appeals to authority are quite reasonable.

---

*   The names of the two experts, Jan Willem Storm van Leeuwen and Phillip Bartlett Smith, are provided in the original article but further research would need to be done to assess their reliability.

ACTIVITY ㉙

Sean appeals to Jamie Oliver's authority. Although Jamie Oliver did present considerable evidence in his very good television programme 'School Dinners', and he is a chef, his expertise is limited to good quality food. He is not an expert on the effects of nutrition on behaviour. Furthermore, Sean uses Oliver to end argument, rather than using his evidence in an argument, which weakens his own case.

'Most parents' are misrepresenting the school's arguments, suggesting that the school is telling them what their children should eat, rather than engaging with the school's good reasons for asking them not to bring junk food. This straw person flaw weakens the parents' case.

Repeated references to children being upset: just because it upsets children, this does not mean that it was wrong. Lots of things which are good for children upset them. However, there does seem to be evidence that the school was heavy-handed and could perhaps have dealt with this issue more sensitively.

Mother Debbie Warton presents a straw person flaw (they want to control our lives). She is inconsistent in saying both that she gives her girls a balanced lunch, and that only half of it is left after the teacher has taken the junk away. She also fails to understand that there are other benefits to nutritious food, such as better behaviour and learning — getting fat is not the only problem with eating junk food.

Dad Kieran May identifies that the school is being hypocritical; he is right that it doesn't make sense to have different rules for school dinners and packed lunches. However, the school's wrong actions do not make it all right for parents to similarly feed their children junk. It could also be questioned whether sausages and chips are as bad as crisps and chocolate: sausages do provide protein, chips do provide carbohydrate, so even though they are fatty, they form the basis of a proper meal.

Grandad Zafar Iqbal, again, appeals to sympathy and lack of popularity of the measure by referring to granddaughter Charlene's tears. He also uses a slippery slope flaw, seeing an extreme end.

Overall, there is a great deal of weak reasoning in this article. So, even though the school has acted in a heavy-handed manner, the parents have not supported their case very well.

ACTIVITY 30

Points you might make include, but are not limited to:

Much of this argument is rant – highly emotive opinions stated one after the other with very little in the way of support given from one idea to the next. There is only a very loose structure of reasons which might support a conclusion and there are two contradictory conclusions: 'Cyclists should not be allowed on our roads,' and, 'These people should be made to pay, and they should be licensed and they should be punished if they do not abide by the regulations of the road.' This seriously weakens any rational support there was. It is not possible to support both of these conclusions at the same time.

The passage begins with an attack on the arguer rather than the argument, and continues this tactic throughout. Most of these attacks are also sweeping generalisations. The generalisation continues throughout the argument and seriously weakens it. It is almost certainly the case that some cyclists (in London and elsewhere) are arrogant and dangerous and do not genuinely care about the environment, etc. However, it is not difficult to demonstrate that there are many calm, quiet cyclists who do abide by road regulations and do try very hard to live an environmentally friendly life, and who do not thrust their cycling credentials down our throats. So strong conclusions drawn on the basis that ALL cyclists are arrogant and dangerous, etc. do not hold up.

In paragraph 2, the author contrasts genteel cyclists of a bygone age with lycra monsters in London. As they refer only to London cyclists, it is possible that the difference is a feature of big cities, or specifically London, and would apply equally to motorists and pedestrians, not just cyclists. The idea of genteel cyclists is also inconsistent with the comment in paragraph 6 about young men being routinely locked up for cycling without lights. It is also an appeal to a nostalgic longing for a better past.

There is a clear equivocation in paragraph 3 in the use of the word 'surroundings' – moving from a green, environmental concern for the world around us to 'surroundings' being angry motorists in traffic jams. Very few environmentalists would extend their concern to this sort of surroundings.

The author returns to attack cyclists with sweeping generalisations about posturing. There is also a misrepresentation in paragraph 4 of what cyclists might think – straw person. Even if the author's claims in this paragraph are right, they give no support to either conclusion – that cyclists should not be allowed on the road, or that they should pay road tax and pay penalties. Being smug and hypocritical is only annoying, not illegal.

Paragraph 5 shows inconsistency; if half these cyclists are being followed by cars, they clearly do pay road taxes. Most cyclists also own cars, so do pay road taxes. Furthermore, not paying road taxes is not a reason to punish cyclists if they do not abide by the regulations of the road. There are good reasons to support this claim, but the author has mentioned none of them.

'Law-abiding' citizens who dream of slashing tyres and jamming sticks in spokes, as described in paragraph 6, clearly demonstrate their own lack of moral superiority, and would probably not belong in their own imagined, gentler era. Two wrongs do not make a right.

Overall, this passage expresses frustration and opinions, but produces very little reasoning, and has not clearly supported a conclusion. It is ranting, rhetorical, inconsistent and flawed. It does arouse emotions in the reader - either of sympathetic outrage or unsympathetic annoyance – but it does not give strong support to a conclusion.

ACTIVITY 31

Answer: C.

ACTIVITY 32

a) Answer: C. **This would be a reason for pharmaceutical companies not to do as much as they can.**

   A   **This is the context of the argument.**

   B   **Reason to support conclusion.**

   D   **Not in the argument.**

b) Answer: B. **The whole point of medicines is to be effective for patients. So pharmaceutical companies should not compromise what they are doing for patients in order to stop abuse.**

   A   **Is not a reason not to try to stop people abusing prescription drugs.**

   C   **This should be an additional measure, not a reason not to try to stop people tampering.**

   D   **This is not a good reason to stop them harming themselves with legal drugs.**

ACTIVITY 33

a) The assumed counter claim is that 'happiness is a fuzzy, unmeasurable concept which cannot be taken seriously.'

b) The author raises the objection that the emotional life of citizens is no business of the state, but dismisses it by saying that this concept is crumbling. Those who believe that the state should have no role in our emotional lives would argue that the concept should not be allowed to crumble; the author has not answered this point.

c) The idea of the nanny state controlling our lives is a common response to attempts by the state to regulate life, so it is important for the author to anticipate and deal with it. Her response is mixed. She suggests that, because the church has lost sway and there is little social solidarity, we have little concept of personal happiness. This in itself is not a reason for the state to intervene. It may be better if people find new understandings of happiness of their own accord. If the state is part of the problem, then it does have a duty to be part of the solution. This does not, however, mean that it should correct the wrongs it does — it could stop doing the wrong. So, the author's response to this counter argument does provide justification for the state to be part of the solution but does not justify direct interference in personal freedom.

ACTIVITY 34

a) It is likely that shouting at my friend will make her feel bad. However, it is unlikely that shouting will stop her eating chocolate, especially as she probably already knows why she shouldn't eat so much. So the support for the conclusion is quite weak.

b) It is possible that using WiFi wine glasses could allow long-distance couples to have a shared experience, but it is not definite. Even if couples do feel this way, it may not be enough to prevent them from growing emotionally distant. If they do not become as emotionally distant, they probably are less likely to split up. But the limited nature of the shared experience is probably not enough to counteract the difficulties of living apart for many people. So the support for the main conclusion is quite weak.

c) Genetic engineering will not necessarily lead to **all** people being more intelligent, healthy, beautiful AND emotionally stable. Genetic engineering is complex, and can only work with genes that are there. It can also only work with traits that are genetically determined. It may be that there is a choice between intelligence and emotional stability, for example, or that the environment people grow up in still affects their stability. It may be that there will be an engineered race of super humans, and 'natural humans' who are always at war. So it would not necessarily be a positive consequence. The argument also ignores any negative consequences, so gives only weak support to the conclusion, that we should promote the legalisation of human genetic engineering.

ACTIVITY 35

a) Answer: D

A doesn't mean that my mind isn't like a pilot who always flies the same plane. B is a similarity. C is a difference between mind and body, not between the situations.

b) Answer: C. **By taking a situation we are familiar with, and highlighting the similarities with a less familiar situation, the comparison makes the difficulties of being an astronaut seem more comprehensible.**

   A   **Comparing the situation of being in a reality TV show and on a shuttle to Mars says nothing about their relative importance. It just highlights some similarities.**

   B   **This answer focuses on one of many aspects, and ignores other reasons why people might want either to go to Mars or to be on reality TV.**

   D   **No – it simply says that there are similar psychological effects of being shut in a small space together, whether in space or not.**

ACTIVITY 36

The argument has limited success in supporting its main conclusion that, 'We should enjoy all that it [the England flag] can offer.'

In the first paragraph, the author anticipates the **counter argument**, that the flag of St George is associated with violent nationalism and racism. The suggestion that this is believed by a 'group of hard-core grumpies' is an attack on the arguer rather than the argument. It is also a rhetorical move to suggest that this is an unreasonable attitude, and if you agree with it, you must be a grumpy.

The second paragraph answers the counter argument with some effectiveness. By suggesting that the meaning of the flag is not set in stone, so it can be changed, and suggesting that we do not wish to give victory to the racists, it does reduce the force of the counter argument.

The **hypothetical reasoning** in the second paragraph, however, assumes that there are positive reasons for rallying round our national flag that might be denied to us by the racist connotations of the flag. It is unclear how the racists gain by everyone else's rejection of overt nationalist behaviour, like flag waving. It seems unlikely that such flag waving will not include racist or nationalistic elements. So, although this paragraph does reduce the force of the counter argument, this reasoning provides little support for the intermediate conclusion that, 'this alone is reason to embrace the flag of St George.'

The third paragraph is rhetorical rather than reasoned. It is a good point that a flag should draw diverse groups of the English together, but there are no reasons and no evidence to suggest that this does happen. The paragraph gives us images and emotions, but no reasoning. There is no reason why a flag that unites some people does not exclude others. The emotive imagery of St George and the Dragon does not give us reason to see young people fighting racism rather than each other — although it is a nice image. These two images are metaphors rather than analogies; they superimpose one image on another rather than saying that there are two situations which are so similar we can draw the same conclusions about them.

In the final paragraph, there is a further **counter argument**, which uses an **analogy**. It is suggested that flag waving months in advance of a major football championship is like putting your Christmas tree up months before Christmas. This seems a strong analogy — both the flag waving and the Christmas tree become ostentatious and meaningless; symbols used for their own sake rather than for any deeper meaning. However, it does not oppose the general idea of using the flag of St George as a symbol of Englishness. The analogy shows that the symbol is being used in a way which empties it of useful meaning. So the author has picked a counter argument which doesn't really oppose their main line of reasoning. They also dismiss it with straw person reasoning, suggesting that the grumpies (repeat of the attacking the arguer) have no serious objections, they just don't like joyous celebration, which misrepresents their arguments quite seriously.

There is a further analogy in the final paragraph, which compares the way the flag draws people to share values and unity with the tourist guide's umbrella which shows the way. There may be a similarity, in that the flag can lead people in a particular direction. However, there are many dissimilarities. The flag does not have a guiding hand, unlike a tourist guide's umbrella. The values associated with the flag are not decided on by a guide figure; they are an accumulation of everything that is thought and felt by all those who use it. As the author has said earlier, these values can change; they are not necessarily good values. So it would be very bad if people sheepishly followed the flag without considering the values attached to it. They may find themselves supporting racists after all.

So, there is some support in the argument for the intermediate conclusion that ' the growing acceptance of our national flag is overwhelmingly positive.' However, we have seen only that it can be positive, not that it is overwhelmingly positive. The move to the main conclusion, that 'we should enjoy all it can offer' is even less strong. We should perhaps enjoy unity and a celebration of diversity as symbolised by the flag; but even the author accepts that the flag has offered a symbol for violent nationalists and that we should not support this part of what the flag can offer.

Glossary

Analogy – a form of argument which uses parallel situations to encourage the audience to accept a conclusion

Argument – an attempt to persuade an audience (readers or listeners) to accept a conclusion by giving reasons to support that conclusion

Assumption – an unstated step which is essential to an argument

Conclusion – a claim which is supported by reasons, which we are supposed to accept after reading an argument

Conflation – bringing different concepts together and treating them as the same

Counter argument – an opposing argument which is shown to be wrong to strengthen the author's argument

Draw a conclusion – to decide what evidence means and what conclusion can be supported by the evidence or reasons

Entail – to have as a necessary consequence

Equivocation – changes in meaning from one use of a word to the next within an argument

Evidence – facts, figures, statistics and specific information used to support a general reason

Explanation – tells how or why something happens but does not persuade listeners or readers to agree with anything

Flaw of causation – a flaw in reasoning which assumes that if two things happen at the same time or one after the other, one of them must have caused the other. However, this is not enough to infer a causal link

Generalisation – drawing a general conclusion from specific evidence

Hasty generalisation – a generalisation which draws a general conclusion from insufficient evidence, often moving from one to all

Hypothetical claim – an 'if … then' sentence which looks at the possible consequences of an event or action

Inconsistency – parts of the argument which pull in different directions, or which would support different conclusions; often both cannot be true at the same time

Infer – to draw conclusions; to consider what is implied by evidence. To decide what the next step is; what can be supported by the evidence or reasons

Intermediate conclusion – a claim which is supported by reasons but which gives support to a further conclusion

Principle – a claim which applies beyond the immediate circumstances of an argument and generally provides a guide to action or belief

Reason – normally a general statement which supports a conclusion by giving us grounds or information which helps us to believe, accept or agree with the conclusion

Reasoning – a thread of persuasive thought, connected in a logical manner

Relevance – has special meaning in Critical Thinking. It means something which is precisely focused on the reason or conclusion it is supporting. Just being about the same topic does not make information relevant to the conclusion

Reliable evidence – evidence that comes from a source which is reputable, authoritative and without a clear vested interest to mislead

Representative evidence – evidence based on a sample which is large enough for the results to be applied more generally

Responding to a counter argument – this involves showing that the counter argument is weak or irrelevant or can be answered. Then it will strengthen your own argument by removing opposition

Rhetorical persuasion – persuades through use of words and emotive language rather than good reasons

Strands of reasoning – developed lines of thought, possibly with evidence, examples, reasons and intermediate conclusion(s)

Sustained hypothetical reasoning – reasoning in which an author looks at a chain of 'ifs' and their consequences, or a long look at the consequences of one 'if'

Sweeping generalisation – a generalisation that moves from many to all, creating a stereotype

Syllogism – a traditional argument structure. It applies a general statement to a particular situation

Valid – in a valid argument, the conclusion must be true if the reasons are true

Verify – to check, or use extra information to confirm a claim or conclusion

Index

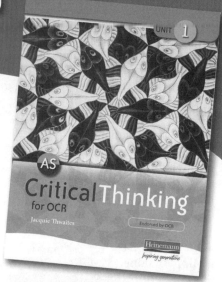